A Writer's Story

A Writer's Story

FROM LIFE TO FICTION

Marion Dane Bauer

Clarion Books/New York

Clarion Books
a Houghton Mifflin Company imprint
215 Park Avenue South, New York, NY 10003
Text copyright © 1995 by Marion Dane Bauer

Type is 11.25/15 Trump Mediaeval
Book design by Carol Goldenberg

Printed in the USA

Library of Congress Cataloging-in-Publication Data
Bauer, Marion Dane.
A writer's story : from life to fiction / by Marion Dane Bauer.
p. cm.
Summary: The author explores the influences that led her to
become a writer including the importance of inspiration.
ISBN 0-395-72094-X   PA ISBN 0-395-75053-9
1. Bauer, Marion Dane—Biography—Juvenile literature. 2. Women
authors, American—20th century—Biography—Juvenile literature. 3.
Children's stories—Authorship—Juvenile literature. [1. Bauer, Marion
Dane. 2. Authors, American. 3. Women—Biography.] I. Title.
PS3552.A8363Z476 1995
813'.54—dc20
[B]   94-48800
CIP   AC

BP 10 9 8 7 6 5 4 3 2 1

For my mother,
Elsie Hempstead Dane Barker,
with love

Contents

A Writer's Story

Introduction

$\mathcal{A}$ debate has long flourished among professional writers. "Can writing be taught?" they ask one another. "No," many say, "it cannot." What they mean is that the creative energy that makes for exceptional writing must come from within the writer. No teacher, however gifted, can impose or supply it from without.

But writing fiction, like every other creative act, requires a fine balance between the creative energy we commonly call inspiration and craft. Certainly the craft of writing can be—and is—successfully taught. My book *What's Your Story? A Young Person's Guide to Writing Fiction* is a case in point. It concentrates on the basics of good story writing: characters, theme, plot, point of view, beginnings and endings, dialogue, story tension, revision. The book says little, however, about the other side of the balance. What are the sources of a writer's creative energy? How do we recognize inspiration when it comes to us? How can that energy best be translated from the writer's life to the page?

These kinds of questions are, of course, exactly what the doubters are thinking of when they maintain that writing cannot be taught. As a longtime writing teacher, I've tried to present my students with solid, comprehensible information about the mechanics of building effective stories and have tended to leave inspiration to the random workings of their own psyches.

And yet, the longer I work as a writer myself, the more I am aware that my own creative process—while certainly not tightly controlled—isn't random at all. I have learned to mine my psyche, to use what happens around and within me to make my stories.

This transformation of raw material into stories occurs on many levels. On the deepest, least conscious one, I seem to have little choice but to try, yet again, to resolve the most fundamental issues of my own childhood. Closer to the surface is the intentional openness I maintain each time I pick up a newspaper or go to the theater or simply pause to examine the ordinary moments of my own daily life. Always, there might be a story idea waiting.

I have managed to write stories, day after day, for more than twenty years—and I hope to be able to go on doing so for many more—precisely because I have begun to understand where my own creative energy comes from and how best to make use of it. And yet I still don't know how to teach others to tap into that place in themselves. I can only talk about my own process, about my own life, about the ways in which my stories grow out of my life, and hope that such a frank and honest discussion will help others to discover the places where their own stories begin.

A Writer's Story is written with two distinct audiences in mind. One is the writers, young people and adults, who have found the lessons about craft in *What's Your Story?* valuable. For you I present the other side of the coin, the more personal, less easily quantified process that brings my stories into being.

The other audience is the readers, again of all ages, who have enjoyed my stories and have found themselves asking the questions every writer encounters along the way: "Where did you get that idea? Did it really happen? How do you fill in the details of your plots?" For you I will try to answer these and other questions that have come to me from readers all over the country.

One writer's process can only be a window into the ways in which other writers work. There is no single "right" method for being creative. But my experience as a fiction writer tells me that the deeper I look into myself, the more universal is the experience I find there. And so I dare to believe that the contents of my psyche, the experience of my transformations of life into stories, will be both interesting and useful to others.

This, then, is my story. It is, in fact, the story of my stories. Whether you are a writer or a reader, whether you are a student or a librarian or a professor of children's literature, it is written for you.

1.

Once Upon a Time . . . There Were Stories

For almost as far back as I can remember, I "wanted to write." Or at least I wanted to make stories. It is almost as though I was born with my head stuffed full to overflowing with stories that waited to be told.

Some of my earliest and fondest memories are of playing with my dolls. Not baby dolls. Those were boring. But people dolls, girl and boy dolls, dolls who had adventures and arguments, who went to school and climbed mountains and struggled their way toward endings, happy or otherwise.

Sometimes I used marbles to people my stories. The larger shooters were the adults. The regular marbles were the kids. (I made sure the kids got all the important parts.) In the summer I turned hollyhock blossoms inside out to make beautiful ladies. My cat in a doll's dress and bonnet became an orphan, abandoned on my doorstep. A broom was a palomino stallion. A stick was a knight's sword.

Best of all, when I had a friend at hand, I made up stories for both of us to act out. Our play sometimes got so realistic that if my mental script called for a quarrel—

and what good story is without conflict?—the friend actually got angry with *me*. Then I faced a real test of my ability to bring stories to a happy resolution. For if I wasn't able to work out the story problem before one of us was called home, my friend might even refuse to see me the next day.

Mine was, I suspect, a universal experience, at least for those of us who grow up to be fiction writers. There is, of course, no one "right" background for a writer to emerge from. We must come from as many different kinds of places as exist on this planet. But we are probably all the same in one respect: We grew up with stories constantly spinning in our heads.

I was born and grew up on the outskirts of a small town named Oglesby in north central Illinois. My father was a chemical engineer for a cement mill; my mother, from the time I entered first grade, was a kindergarten teacher in a nearby town. My parents, my older brother, Willis, and I lived in the housing provided for mill workers, close to the dusty, clanging mill. A farmer's field, planted in corn, separated our home from the highway. A woods stood between us and the Vermillion River. The proper term, I suppose, is "hardwood forest," but we always called it a woods and laughed at visitors from Chicago who, inordinately impressed with what was so common to us, called it a forest. (Those who have read my book *On My Honor* will recognize the Vermillion River. Readers of *Rain of Fire* will notice in the above description many of the exact details of Steve's home.)

It was only when, as an adult, I looked back on my childhood that I realized how poor this environment would have seemed to most outsiders. Cement dust sifted down on everything from the smoke that poured out of the mill stack day and night. Nearby switch engines huffed and freight cars slammed into one another as coal was delivered to the mill and cars were filled with cement and taken away. The tiny frame house I was born in was lined up side by side with a dozen or so others, all built from one of two patterns.

But I was proud of the mill, even admired the puffy white smoke that constantly drifted across the sky. It was a cloud during the day; at night, a dark path that blotted the stars. My father, who was responsible for such things, said that when the smoke was white it meant the kilns were burning clean, so I knew it was *good* as well as beautiful. He also maintained that the fine dust that sifted down on us when the smoke passed overhead couldn't possibly be responsible for my mother's sinus headaches. It was, after all, *"clean* dust." Even the rackety trains and the men who worked on them were romantic to my eye, simply more material for the stories that grew in my fertile mind.

It never occurred to me that the four-room house we lived in until I was seven years old was a tight fit for a family of four. Moving to a larger mill house on the other side of the corn field, this one closer to the mill, was merely an adventure, not the long-awaited release it must have been for my parents.

Once we had moved, though, I was delighted to have a spacious screened porch, stairs, and a room of my own with interestingly sloping ceilings and a window overlooking a wooded hill. I rejoiced in the sprawling yard with its lilacs and fruit trees, its grape arbor, and the rope-and-board swings in two different oaks. (One of the oaks stood on a hill, and in its swing a mere touch of the toes to the ground was enough to send me soaring.) And the dense woods that took up where our yard left off were a constant lure . . . and hazard. I was acutely allergic to the poison ivy that grew so abundantly there.

If there was a drawback to this idyllic environment, it was that I was often without playmates. While there happened to be a number of boys in the neighborhood for my brother, who was two years older than I, to play with, during much of the time I was growing up there were no girls. And though I played with my brother—at least when he had nothing better to do—I never found a place in the rough and tumble of the neighborhood boys. So I was often alone. Not lonely, necessarily, but alone. I suppose my stories took the place of friends.

When I started school, however, I was quite unprepared for the sudden wealth of children who surrounded me. Nor were the other children, apparently, prepared for me. First, I didn't live "in town," and therefore I couldn't really belong. Second, my complex inner life probably interfered with my learning the rules for getting along with my peers. Third, I started kindergarten when I was still four and thus was a good part of a year behind many of my classmates, at least socially. (Actually, kindergarten went along reasonably well, but in first grade I was put in with the older, more "advanced" group, and my relationship with my classmates went downhill from there.) Moreover, my mother, who preferred babies to independent children, had encouraged me to stay "little," so I was noticeably and painfully immature in both dress and manner.

It is one thing to be physically isolated. It is something else entirely to be isolated in the midst of one's peers. To be continually on the outside, ignored, sometimes even scorned, creates real loneliness. And there is no question . . . I was an extremely lonely child.

Not long ago I was listening to a presentation by a former student of mine who is now a published children's writer. She spoke of having been a lonely child. Another children's writer sitting next to me leaned over and said, simply, "Weren't we all?" I don't know whether all children's writers had lonely childhoods. Even if most of us did, there are sure to be some who were happy, well-adjusted kids with lots of friends. But I do know that my aloneness—the long hours spent wandering in the woods, dreaming in the crotch of a cherry tree, moving my dolls through various scripts—is part of the richness out of which I now write. Even the loneliness of standing apart from my classmates serves my stories today.

I assume that all human beings who are born with normally functioning brains are born also with the capacity for imagination. Those of us who found ourselves alone, choosing books for friends and interacting with dolls or marbles or hollyhock blossoms, may, however, have had a push toward becoming writers, perhaps particularly writers for children.

When I go into schools to talk about my books, I am drawn to the lonely kids, the outsiders, the ones in whose eyes I glimpse my own remembered isolation. I am drawn especially to the ones who sidle up to me and speak, with longing and even some pain, of the stories they "want to write." And I always wish I could say, "Just wait. I know you're hurting, but the day will come when you can transform what you're feeling now into strength and compassion . . . into stories."

I have never said it, because how can I presume to know anything so personal about someone I have met so briefly? But I never forget those young people either . . . or the older ones whose eyes speak of the same remembered place.

Today the lonely child I once was sits down with me every time I settle, so contentedly, to my work. "I'm here," she says. "Remember me?"

I remember. Because though there is nothing about my present life that could be described as lonely, that girl's pain is part of what has made me the woman I am.

I once played alone out of necessity. These days I work alone by choice.

As a child I was an outcast. My empathy, as an adult, brings me friends.

I used to spend endless hours acting out my longing. It is my privilege now to transform that longing into stories.

Stories that are published and read.

2.

The Child Hole

I have heard it said that we children's authors write to create something that was left out of our own childhoods. That is certainly true of me. And the fact that I am rarely conscious of my longing for that missing part doesn't diminish my reach. When I had published only one or two novels, I used to say, quite blithely, "No one can psychoanalyze me by reading one of my books, because I *never* write autobiographically." (And I don't. I never write about myself in any conscious way. I rarely even draw from events in my own life.) But after I had written several books, I began to discover—and occasionally to hear perceptive readers comment on—some of the patterns my stories repeat. These patterns, I came to realize, reveal me more intimately than the surface facts of my life ever could.

Throughout my childhood, I was well taken care of. All of my material, educational, and health needs were reliably met. My emotional needs fell into a somewhat different category, however. In the first place, my parents were from a generation and a culture (both sides of my family came, at one time or another, from Great

Britain) in which feelings were thought to be not quite *nice*. It wasn't considered proper in my family to display feelings, talk about feelings, or even acknowledge the existence of feelings.

My father was a brilliant man whose college degree was in chemistry. He was also very much a concrete thinker. The stuff of the imagination was, for him, not just inconsequential but something to be scorned. When I was working on a master's degree in literature in my early twenties, he could not comprehend how anyone could study literature. What was there, after all, to learn?

Dad trained my brother and me well. As long as we could carry on a rational argument, whether the subject was politics or our bedtimes, he heard us. But if we—or I should say *I*, because my brother learned to conform to my father's reality much more readily than I—showed emotion of any kind, we encountered his scorn.

The family often gathered at the kitchen table, both for meals and for discussions, and I can still see my father in his usual place. He sat on one side of the table, not at the head, but he dominated nonetheless. "Life," he often said, with deep and bitter conviction, "is a dirty deal." And I, the young romantic, the faithful churchgoer and believer in the almost mystical power of stories, would leap to the defense of life and the universe. (In my stories I am doing so still, taking on my father's dark view of the world, acknowledging it, and wrestling it through to the light.) Neither of us ever managed to convince the other, but because I was a child, I was the one who always met defeat, who ended up leaving the table.

Oh, how clearly I remember the path from the kitchen up the stairs to my room. I can feel, even today, the reverberation of my slammed door, remember the disgraced and disgraceful tears. All because I was the one in the family who descended from logic to *feelings*, over and over and over again. (My mother is also, I believe, very much a feeling person, though her family background had also taught her a profound emotional restraint. She protected herself with silence, simply declining to engage in most of the discussions my brother and I were drawn into.)

Any point raised with my father, even one that attempted to reproduce his own views, brought down a contradiction. I often suspected him of taking the opposing side merely for the pleasure of being contrary, whatever the topic might be. As a consequence, I was an adult before I began to learn that there is a difference between a conversation and an argument. I was also an adult before I had the first glimmerings of understanding that all human beings are feeling creatures, that our feelings are not only right and proper but inevitable, part of our very substance.

Thus I came to my writing with a strong need to explore feelings, to play them out, to legitimize them. The emotional self-control I learned across the kitchen table from my father, or tried valiantly to learn but too often failed at in the end, now gives power to my writing.

I can handle strong material with the restraint he tried to teach me. But now I can arrive, finally, at the moment he wouldn't allow, the moment when the feelings break through the surface. And the satisfaction for me is that I don't have to stomp off to my room in disgrace at the end of the story. Nor do my characters. Joel, in *On My Honor*, can weep in his father's arms. Caitlin, in *A Taste of Smoke*, can grow sentimental over her first kiss . . . even if it is from a ghost. Brad, in *A Question of Trust*, can put aside his anger toward his mother and reach for her again.

Another pattern that emerges again and again in my work is that of the alienated child who finally makes a connection with a parent or parent figure. *Shelter from the Wind* opens with Stacy's running away from home. On the last page of the story, she chooses to return. In *A Dream of Queens and Castles* Diana starts out petulant and angry, resenting being forced to move to England with her mother. By the last chapter she decides, of her own will, to stay, and she and her mother set out to explore together. *On My Honor* begins with Joel's anger and disappointment with his father. It ends not just with Joel's confession, but with a reconciliation between father and son. Joel recognizes that he can't change his father but that, still, his father is there for him.

All of these stories have come, I suppose, out of my own desire for an acceptance and understanding that wasn't available to me within my family. My mother is a taciturn woman, little given to praise or words of affection. The older her children grew, the more difficult it was for her to be intimate with them, either verbally or physically. My father, as I've mentioned, actively discouraged displays of feeling. Even though I always knew that my parents cared about me, I could never get enough concrete experience of that caring to satisfy my craving. I spent my childhood longing for overt approval, if not from them then from some other adult.

I imagine that every adult alive yearns for something his or her growing-up years failed to provide. Human beings and their needs are so complex, parents' as well as children's, that even in the best-functioning families, people fail one another in crucial ways. In fact, I am convinced that every one of us brings into adulthood an unfulfilled place I have heard referred to as a "child hole." It's a place where, however careful and caring our parents might be and have been, there are deep and important needs that weren't met.

The question is, then, what do we do about those needs? Many of us marry and build new families, trying to create for ourselves and our children whatever we missed the first time around. Some of us go into therapy to face the child hole, to understand it and learn to meet its needs for ourselves. Some work with children, trying to do for others what wasn't done for them. A fiction writer, especially one who writes for children, may do all of the above, but he or she also turns to stories. In a story, the needs can be acknowledged, over and over again. They can also be met, at last. The father understands. The mother reveals herself. The older brother or sister reaches out to bridge the gap.

When I first realized that I was playing out this same theme—the child's search for a connection with a parent or parent figure—in every story, I was appalled. How could I go on repeating myself this way? It didn't matter how well written my stories might be. I wanted my work to be varied as well as deep, identifiably mine but not predictable. And I looked at whatever I was working on at the moment of my discovery and saw that, when I got to the last page, "it" was going to happen again. The stepfather would reach out for the son he'd never quite connected with before. The daughter was going to discover her father. Mother and daughter were about to talk.

It's all over! I thought. *I might as well give up. I've said everything I have to say!*

It took me some time—and much discomfort—before I began to understand. This need of mine is the basis for much of the energy that sets my stories in motion. And it can be the basis for as many different kinds of stories as I am capable of writing. So instead of worrying about its familiarity, I now use it. I draw on it more consciously all the time. I turn that longing over, look at its soft underbelly, and ask, for instance, *What if the mother runs away instead of the kid? What if the story is about him trying to bring her home?* And from that I discover *A Question of Trust*. The new stories continue to grow.

In the years since that first disturbing discovery, I still find myself fretting sometimes. Is *A Question of Trust* too much like *Rain of Fire*? Or perhaps it's *Shelter from the Wind* it reminds me of more. I remember a column I read in the magazine *The Writer* when I was still an aspiring writer myself. The columnist, an old pro with many books to her name, spoke with quiet envy of new writers. So much material yet untouched! At the time I was so in awe of her—so many books!—that I could hardly comprehend what she was complaining about. Now I understand it only too well.

I keep concentrating on stretching, trying to vary my work. I'm exploring stories for younger children, picture-book texts like *When I Go Camping with Grandma*, *Jason's Bears*, and *If You Were Born a Kitten*; an easy reader, *Alison's Wings*. In order to extend myself further I've taken on fantasies such as *Touch the Moon* and ghost stories like *Ghost Eye* and *A Taste of Smoke*. And I have discovered something curious along the way: The more my stories change, the more they stay the same.

As I was writing the final moment of *Ghost Eye*—when Popcorn the cat finally turns to Melinda, his young owner, for the first time—I found myself laughing out loud. The end felt exactly right. It could have been Steve reconciling with his older brother in *Rain of Fire*, Leslie reaching out to her mother in *Like Mother, Like Daughter*, Stacy returning home in *Shelter from the Wind*. For better or for worse, I had written, once more, a Marion Dane Bauer story.

A child's need to connect with a parent or parent figure is not my only theme, though I suspect it will always be my strongest. In fact, I've had occasion lately to wonder, *If that child hole is finally filled, will I still be able to write? Will the stories in my head stop demanding to be played out?*

And so I push myself. I write *A Taste of Smoke*, in which the renewal of Caitlin's connection with her older sister seems to be the impetus for the story. Familiar stuff. And yet the resolution moves beyond the reconciliation of the two sisters to a connection of another kind. When I wrote the scene in which Caitlin kissed her ghostly boyfriend, I didn't find myself laughing, but I surely did smile.

Well, Marion, I said to myself, *it took you a lot of years to arrive at this place. Now you've finally moved beyond a child's need for acceptance by a parent to a need of another kind. I know he's only a ghost, but at least your main character has been kissed . . . at last!*

And then I turned around and wrote *A Question of Trust,* in which a child, again, seeks a parent.

It is probably the nature of a child hole that it will never be entirely filled, however long our therapy, however many stories we write. Can you imagine such a life, anyway? A world in which every hunger is satisfied, every longing resolved? How dull it would be!

As I write this, there are still more stories dancing in my head. There is one about a fifteen-year-old boy whom I especially love. His name is Luke, and he talks to me constantly, saying the most outrageous things. He considers himself a truthseeker, and he has decided that he will be either a contemplative monk or a reporter for the *National Enquirer,* depending on whether *he* determines that God exists. Luke is in love with his English teacher, who happens to be not only his teacher and middle-aged, but a lesbian as well. An impossible connection, of course. A totally impossible child-parent connection.

Which makes me understand why I am writing this book instead of that story. I know Luke's story problem, but as yet I have no ending. Reconciliation? Understanding between the two? Perhaps, but there must be something more. What becomes of Luke's desire when the relationship can't satisfy it for him? And how do I tap into the energy that drives my stories if the connection with the parent figure can never happen?

I could use the word *inspiration* for this process of finding the impetus for my stories at my own core, but I prefer to call it *energy*. *Inspiration* sounds like such a rare phenomenon, as though in order to write stories one must be prone to exotic experiences withheld from more ordinary folk. But we all have *energy*, we all recognize energy when it rises within us.

The child hole, *my* child hole, will, I presume, continue to energize my stories. I may even discover recesses of it that I haven't yet explored. Perhaps it will be Luke, engaged in his impossible search, who will teach me. Or maybe there is simply an outer story—one I haven't explored fully enough yet—between Luke and his mother, and this story, too, will remain true to my familiar pattern.

Everyone has a child hole, even the very young. It may be more difficult for young people to use that place to energize their writing because they are living deep in their child hole, right now. In fact, it may feel like the entire world to them. However, that unfulfilled place constitutes, for young people as well as for adults, the core of their longing, and longing is what fiction is about. The main character must *want* something, and then he must struggle to get it.

When I am working with students of all ages who want to write but can't find *what* they want to write, I always begin by asking them what they like to read, what they like to do, what excites them, scares them, makes them sad. It's a search that begins with the superficial and moves tentatively toward that deep inner place where, suddenly, something feels *important*. It is that feeling of importance that energizes a story.

We writers can use our own longing—and frequently do—without ever having to understand or analyze it. That is why our stories are often wiser than we are. But we must feel the longing to be able to use it. And in my experience, that feeling takes the form of a rush of energy whenever I stumble across an idea—in my life, in the newspaper, in my imagination—that might work for a story. I rarely ask myself why an idea excites me, what it has to do with my life. That is, more often, a subject to be examined after the story is written . . . if at all. I can only be grateful for the child hole out of which my stories are born . . . and go on writing.

Kids often ask me, "How many more books are you going to write?" And I always say, "As long as my brain keeps functioning, as long as there is someone out there wanting to read my stories, I expect to go on making books."

How else can I keep in touch with all those forbidden feelings? How else can I keep learning who I am?

3.

To Tell the Truth

I was lied to as a child. Now, it may be—in fact, I consider it very likely—that I wasn't lied to any more than other children of my generation. When I was growing up, in the forties and early fifties, it was considered part of every adult's responsibility to "protect" children, even from the truth. Especially from any truth that made adults uncomfortable.

I never liked being lied to. And by the time I was an adult and could look back to see how much information had been withheld along the way, even how much direct misinformation I had been given, I was pretty indignant about the whole thing.

Sex, birth, divorce, death. None of these topics was considered fit for children. Which meant that when such subjects entered our awareness, we had to fill in the blanks on our own. And oh, how those blanks got filled in!

I remember very clearly the bright summer morning when it occurred to me, for the first time, to ask my mother, "But how does the baby get *into* the mommy's tummy?" (I don't know exactly how old I was, but I

remember the conversation's taking place in the first little house we all lived in, so I had to have been under
seven.)

My mother was in the kitchen doing "mother
things," and she answered very rapidly, without turning
to look at me, "They take something out of the father
and put it into the mother."

I thought about that for a moment. They *take something out of the father and put it into the mother.* How
did *they* do that?

"Is it an operation?" I asked.

"No," my mother said as she stirred a pot.

"Then what do they do?" I demanded to know.

My mother's face slammed shut.

I was old enough to understand that I had stumbled
into a subject that would not be discussed, so I took the
piece of information I had been given and went outside
to sort it out myself.

My mother had said that the baby wasn't put into the
mother's tummy by means of an operation, but she had
to be wrong about that. There was no other explanation
that made any sense. And in a very short time, I had
worked it all out.

People got married, and then, of course, they went on
a honeymoon. I knew all about honeymoons. But it was
perfectly clear that something happened between the
wedding and the honeymoon about which, for whatever
reason, adults preferred not to speak.

After the wedding, I decided, the young couple
stopped by the doctor's office for a bit of surgery. The
doctor cut open the man's belly and removed something. I even knew what the thing he removed looked

like. It was round and pink and glistening, and it had bumps on it. It had a bump for each baby the couple would eventually have. Then the doctor cut open the woman's belly, put the thing inside, sewed them both up again, and sent the couple off on their honeymoon. Later, at times I assumed to be unpredictable, one of these bumps would mature into a baby and pop out, and the husband and wife would cry, "How wonderful! We have a baby!"

There was just one aspect of this carefully constructed scenario that disturbed me, apart from anticipating the discomfort of that surgery one day for myself. I had, in a very general way, picked up the information that when couples got married they didn't seem to know how many children they would have in the course of their lives together. And I thought, *Isn't it just like grown ups? They're so dumb. All they'd have to do is count the bumps, and then they'd know!*

It occurred to me, of course, that in the midst of being cut open and sewn up again, neither the husband nor the wife might feel like counting the bumps. But surely the doctor could do it, couldn't he? Then, at the very least, the couple would start out knowing how many bedrooms they were going to need.

The solid scenario I built from the limited information my mother gave me was typical of the way I created explanations of all sorts of important life events. My mother's half-truth was also typical of the way children of my generation were dealt with far too often. We were left to work out some of the most important facts about human experience on our own.

I remember being lied to even more directly. It

occurred to me one day that I hadn't seen my godfather's wife for a long time. In actual fact, the couple had been divorced, but the subject had never been mentioned in front of me. "Didn't Dr. S. used to have a wife?" I asked, feeling a bit bewildered. My mother simply said, "No."

And so my very sense of reality was challenged. If he didn't have a wife, why did I remember her? My godfather was our family doctor, and his wife had been his office nurse. I could remember clearly the time he set my broken arm and she kept trying to get me to laugh by putting my velvet bonnet on her head. (I thought she was being silly and only cried harder.) Could my memory be completely wrong?

As a young adult looking back on such incidents, I felt betrayed. It took me some time to realize that I had suffered from a social phenomenon, not an intentional betrayal on the part of my own parents. But those kinds of experiences turned me into a conscious and very passionate truthteller. My own daughter, in fact, finds me "pathologically honest."

I'm not the kind of honest that comments on ugly hats or tells students that their writing is terrible. But I am quite incapable, especially when I am talking to a child, of answering a direct question with a less-than-direct answer.

One Christmas morning, when my son, Peter, was three and a half years old, he asked me, "Mommy, did Santa Claus really tiptoe into my room and put those things in my stocking or did you do it?" And I admitted that I had done it. It was the only answer I knew how to give. I went on to tell him, of course, about Santa Claus as an "idea," a spirit of giving, but at three and a half he wasn't interested in any of that. He had the concrete information he wanted.

As a consequence of my truthfulness, my daughter Beth-Alison, who was two years younger, never had a chance to believe in Santa Claus, even for a moment. Her brother was right there to tell her what was what. Years later she told me that my answer to Peter was the worst thing I'd ever done as a parent. If that truly was the worst, I've decided she was pretty lucky. However, given my daughter's experience and the very different child hole she has been left with, she has turned out to be a reliably honest woman but not a "pathological" truthteller.

I suspect that many other writers of realistic children's fiction—especially those of my generation—have the same need to be truthful as I. I've heard Judy Blume say, "Truth never hurts children, but withholding information does," and I've smiled to myself, knowing exactly what she is saying, what she is feeling. It leaves me wondering how Judy's mother answered her when she first asked how the baby gets into the mommy's tummy.

And so when I was writing my first novels, *Foster Child* and *Shelter from the Wind*, I was on an intense mission. I would right the wrongs that had been done to me. I would tell the truth, especially about those topics not usually discussed with children.

I have rarely had a young reader object to the topics of my stories or to the truths I insist on revealing, even though they are sometimes uncomfortable ones. From time to time, however, adults object to one of my books with the same passion that I bring to my truthtelling. And as a consequence, occasionally one of my stories is banned . . . or at least is threatened with the possibility.

I have been asked how I feel about having one of my novels banned. Actually, I feel surprisingly little, except that my book is in good company. It seems that the best of our literature is often banned while the worst comes and goes without eliciting a great deal of excitement.

I also believe that a banning is not about me, even when those who object to what I have written take presumptive leaps from my fiction to my life. Those who wanted to ban *Foster Child* when it was first published, for instance, usually assumed that the book's author was against religion. I used to take great pleasure in pointing out that not only was I not against religion but was, in those years, a clergy-wife and dependent upon the church for my daily living. What I was objecting to, in fact, when I wrote that novel was the *abuse* of religion.

I don't support book banning, of course, but I do support something else that isn't encouraged often enough. Every reader has a right to disagree with any writer's "truth." My truth, whether it is the careful depiction of a birth scene or my convictions about religion, is spelled in my stories with a very small *t*. That means it's mine, my perception of the world, my decision about what should be spoken and how.

Readers who want to ban books are assuming that books are—or should be or can be—about Truth with a capital *T*. They believe that books should be written only about what everyone can agree is right and real and appropriate. But the book that everyone would agree is True has yet to be written. And if it could exist, it would lack that individual passion that makes stories come alive.

My truths come out of my individual experience. They may reinforce the truths of my readers' lives . . . or contradict them entirely. For instance, here is a unique experience of mine that had a profound impact on the themes I have felt compelled to explore, especially in my early novels.

As I have already mentioned, I was a child who lived in her imagination. Never to the point that I didn't know the difference between fantasy and reality, but certainly to the point that what was going on inside my head often felt a whole lot more important than what was going on in the world around me. Throughout my childhood and even into early adulthood, I occupied myself constantly with stories that I wove inside my head. But then I woke up one morning in my mid-twenties and found my head empty, the stories gone!

I have never known exactly what prompted my head to empty so abruptly, and at first I was bereft. But gradually, without all that commotion in my brain, I found myself able to turn my attention more effectively to the world around me, and eventually my stories returned and became something I could take charge of, something I could actually begin to put on paper.

That experience of loss had a strong impact on me, and it is one I played out repeatedly in my early novels as an important "truth." However wonderful fantasy may be, the resolutions of my stories proved, it must be given up so that one may live in the real world. In *Shelter from the Wind*, Stacy pretends that she is going to find her mother, but accepts her real stepmother at the story's conclusion. Renny, in *Foster Child*, dreams about her nonexistent father, but finally turns to the foster parents who are there for her. In *Tangled Butterfly*, Michelle creates a soothing grandmother who talks to her, but gives her up in the end.

Once, after I had mentioned to a class this repeated—and quite unconscious—theme of mine, a student replied, "It's different for me. When I'm writing, I'm always saying, 'You don't have to accept reality. Try fantasy!'"

Whose stories are true? Mine or my student's? The answer depends on who you are, what you need to hear at a particular moment in your life. Both could be true . . . or neither . . . or one on one day and the other on another.

One of the first things every child should learn about the books he is read on his parents' laps is to challenge them. To ask whether the cows he knows jump over the moon. To consider whether it's an interesting thought anyway, even if it doesn't happen. To wonder whether the Giving Tree did well in giving itself up so totally for the selfish boy/man. To discuss whether we really do have to give up our fantasies in order to live in the real world.

I remember with great clarity a picture book from my early childhood. I don't know the author or title, and I haven't been successful in locating it again, but I still react to its message. It was about a small train that, instead of running along the track the way all the big trains did, preferred to run through the meadow to enjoy the freedom and the flowers. The big trains objected, of course. Trains were meant to run on tracks, not through meadows. And by the end of the story, they had brought the small train back into line. They installed stoplights all over the meadow, so wherever the small train went, he was forced to stop. Since it was no longer any fun to run through the meadow, the small train went back onto the track and never left it again.

The message of the book wasn't lost on me. *Conform. Do what adults tell you to, whether it makes sense or not. Don't ever go off the track, however beautiful the flowers may be.* I was furious with what I know now was a good, healthy fury. *What harm was the little train doing?* I asked myself. *Why did the big trains care that he was leaving the track to run through the meadow?* There wasn't the slightest indication in the story that the small train was hurting the meadow or even that he had other work he was supposed to be doing. The big trains simply objected to his enjoying something they weren't free enough to enjoy themselves.

I also thought the small train was foolish to be intimidated by the stoplights. If he had the courage to go off the track to start with, why didn't he have the courage to ignore those meaningless lights? I could find no immediate answer to either of my concerns . . . but one gradually dawned.

Maybe the author's truth and mine were different.

Maybe his words didn't have to be true for me even if they were set down in a book. Maybe *my* truth was valid for *my* life, no matter what was true for the little train!

What makes books powerful is the passion of the writers who produce them. We write what we believe. Each of us. And that makes our stories as individual and various as we are. As a reader, I have found that the antidote for a piece of fiction with which I do not agree is to move on to another author, another piece of fiction, another truth.

No one told me that I didn't have to like what happened to the little train, that I didn't have to believe that the big trains were right. I figured it out for myself out of my own anger. But I can remember turning from that story to another, one that confirmed my own truth. It was the story of Ferdinand, the gentle bull, who *didn't* do what the world insisted he should. When he was expected to fight, he stayed in his meadow and smelled the flowers, exactly what I thought the little train should have done. Of course, there were those who objected to *The Story of Ferdinand*, because it supported pacifism in a time of war, but they had other stories in which to find what they were seeking.

We are all taught to read at an early age. I wish we were also taught to *think* about what we read, to challenge it, to weigh it against our own lives. That wish applies even and especially to stories, because they reach so much deeper than mere facts. They reach into an author's most private truths and give us each an opportunity to examine our own.

4.

The Secret Revealed

"Where do your story ideas come from?" The question comes up again and again, from adults and young people alike. And when I have finished giving my very best answer, the questioner is often clearly unsatisfied. "But where do your story ideas really come from?" someone asks yet again. It is as though we writers are suspected of harboring secrets, hiding a key to a box, the contents of which we are unwilling to share.

The answer I have given in the last two chapters is, I promise, *the* answer, at least for me. It is the deepest I can go. I am writing to answer needs from my own childhood, to fill that child hole. I write out of old hurts I am attempting to heal. I write out of my deepest convictions, sometimes out of convictions I am not fully aware of myself. That is why I turn to stories to play them out. In fact, if there is anyone who stands to learn from my novels, it is I. When I look back at my own stories after they are written—or hear thoughtful evaluations of them from my readers—I often discover truths I hadn't realized I knew. Especially truths about my own psyche.

But that answer speaks to the impetus behind my stories, the energy that makes them happen. It doesn't speak to their content, and it is the content, I suppose, that my questioners really want to know about. "Where did you get the idea for *A Dream of Queens and Castles*, for *Face to Face*?" they are asking. And especially, "Did it happen to you?"

I have never yet written a novel that literally recounts episodes from my own life, though fragments of my life invariably make their way into the details of my stories. And I have never yet populated a story with people I know, though, of course, all I can base my characters on is what I know of myself and the people I have loved and struggled with over the years.

I'll use *Shelter from the Wind* to explain what I mean. It was my very first novel, or at least my first to be published. *Foster Child* was actually written first but published second.

In a more obvious way than any of my other novels, *Shelter from the Wind* is about a child's search for a parent, the theme I discussed in Chapter 2. Here, the search is overt. Stacy runs away from home in order to punish her father, to make him "sorry," but also because she has decided to find her mother, who had abandoned the family when Stacy was very young. Stacy knows only that her mother lives somewhere "in the Rockies," so the search is not exactly a logical one, but it is passionately felt.

Once we have touched on this psychological base for the story, however, a base of which I was entirely unconscious at the time I was writing, the connection to my life seems to end. Few of the major facts of Stacy's story come from my own experience. Stacy's parents are divorced, and she resents her stepmother. My parents were never divorced, so I had no stepparents. Stacy is growing up in the Oklahoma panhandle. I grew up in Illinois. Stacy is jealous over a soon-to-be-born baby. I was the youngest in my family and often longed for a baby brother or sister. Stacy's mother is an alcoholic. My parents and the other adults I knew best when I was a child rarely touched intoxicating beverages of any kind.

This lack of connection between fiction and actuality probably explains why writers' story ideas seem like a mystery to many people. If I could say that something similar had happened to me when I was twelve years old, then everyone's questions would be answered. Or at least they would seem to be answered.

And yet many of the details that bring Stacy's story to life do come from my experience. Stacy runs away from home. I never did such a thing. Still—and this is what matters—I can remember what it feels like to *want* to run away. And perhaps for a writer the wanting is more important than the doing.

For several years when I was young I had a friend named Betty with whom I played, and she and I often made plans for running away together. The idea, as I recall, was mine, but Betty always agreed that whenever I was ready, "summer or winter, night or day," she would gladly go with me. Well, one day I was ready. I don't remember what prompted my decision—some injustice, real or imagined, I suppose—but I do know that my mind was made up.

I wrote a note and tucked it away someplace where

my parents would be sure to find it, though not too soon. I didn't want to be embarrassed by being hauled back home before I'd made a proper escape. I packed a bandanna with whatever seemed essential, tied the corners together, put a stick through the knot, and slung the whole thing over my shoulder, hobo style. (There is no question about it, I was a romantic.) And then I went over to Betty's house and called her out. (When I was a child, kids rarely knocked on doors. We stood outside one another's houses and called.) Betty came to the door, and I told her that I was ready to run away and that I wanted her to go with me. Her face fell. "Gee," she said, "I'm sorry. I want to. I really do. But I can't. I'm eating supper."

Supper! I thought. *Supper? How could supper be more important than her promise to me?* I turned away, feeling abandoned . . . and a bit hungry, too. (Her reason for not going made me realize that I hadn't yet had *my* supper.) But what else could I do except go on with my plan? My note was written, my bandanna packed, my mind made up. And so, entirely alone, I headed up the gravel lane that ran alongside the mill.

It was about a quarter of a mile to the two-lane highway that connected our home to the rest of the world, and that part of the walk was easy. I walked it every school day on my way to and from the bus. I walked it when my brother and I went into town to a movie or to the community pool.

But once I had reached the highway, I was confronted with a difficult decision. If I turned right I would go into town . . . where I would inevitably be seen by people who knew my parents. People who might ask what I was doing, strolling along far from home with a hobo pack over my shoulder. If I turned left, I would go out into the country. Miles and miles into the country. And though I had less worry about being seen there, I also hadn't the vaguest idea what I would do in the country or where, in all that vast stretch of woods and fields, I might want to go. So I stood at the end of my lane, unable to move in any direction at all.

A car rumbled past and then another. After a short time, I began to feel conspicuous, standing there next to the highway with my hobo pack over my shoulder, so I went and stood behind a tree. Another car or two passed, and I began to feel distinctly foolish, standing behind a tree next to the highway with my hobo pack over my shoulder, and so I turned around and walked back home. I tore up the note lest my righteous indignation become a matter for ridicule. I unpacked. I ate my supper. And that was my entire experience as a runaway.

But the important thing is that when I came to write *Shelter from the Wind*, I knew exactly what it felt like to want to run away. It was the helpless rage, the remembered conviction, however inaccurate, that my parents "didn't care," that gave me my story. And once I was in touch with all that, I had only to say "what if" to begin to write.

What if a girl who felt the way I had actually did run away? What if she stormed out the door and kept going? What if she walked so far that she didn't have a choice about turning back that same day? What would happen next?

Other details of the story come from places that

evoked strong feelings in me. (Place is important to my stories, and I always choose a setting that I have known and loved, though that setting may have no connection with my own childhood.) Old Ella's wedding tree was based on the mimosa tree that grew in my backyard during the brief period when, as an adult, I did live in a small town in the Oklahoma panhandle. That beautiful tree, blooming at the time I moved in, was a real comfort to a young mother and wife who found herself a stranger in a not entirely friendly place. And so when I began writing the story, it bloomed for me again.

The checkered beam in Ella's cabin came from one I'd seen in an abandoned homesteader's cabin out on the Oklahoma prairie. It, too, was painted in precise checks. And the day I stepped into the ruins of that old cabin, I found myself transfixed by that checkered beam. I had an instant image of someone standing on a chair or a box and reaching up painstakingly, day after day, to decorate the little house. In a land so vast, the need for beauty that is human-sized can be incredibly strong. *Somebody*, I thought, *spent a* long *winter here!*

The checks on the beam in the abandoned cabin were black and white. The ones in Ella's home are described as being like the checkered red and white of "Mamma's tablecloth at home." Once one of my "feeling memories" enters a story, it belongs to my characters, and it is transformed to suit their needs.

Another element in *Shelter from the Wind* came from a different part of my life entirely. Ella's white German shepherd, Nimue, was based on my son's dog, also named Nimue. (While I have never used one of my children or anyone else I know in my books, I steal shame-lessly from my pets. After all, they can't read, so how can they ever accuse me of "getting it wrong"?)

The real Nimue was named for the white fairy in the King Arthur stories, because Peter and I were reading every version of those stories we could find when the gangly white pup joined our family. And as in my book, Peter's Nimue had puppies, though never by a mate named Merlin. The first time the real Nimue was due to deliver, I went to the library to read up on how pup-pies are born. I had been involved with the birth of kit-tens, but never puppies, and I wanted to be prepared.

One piece of information I gathered was that, when all the pups were born, I should check to make sure none had a cleft palate. If one did, the text told me in the no-nonsense manner of instructional books, I was to slip it away when the mother wasn't watching and destroy it. A puppy with a cleft palate can't suck, the book explained, so if I didn't intervene, the new puppy would starve to death, slowly and painfully.

Could I kill a newborn puppy? I asked myself, the enormity of the act striking me with the force of a blow. I didn't question that it was what should be done. How could anyone stand by and watch a new little creature suffer? But could I, personally, do such a thing? I still don't know whether I could or not, because, to my great relief, I was never tested. Peter's Nimue had two litters before she was spayed, and every one of her puppies was perfect.

In real life, no one goes out looking for problems. *No one* says, "Wouldn't it be interesting if one of the pups was born with a cleft palate and I had to kill it to stop its suffering?" But stories require problems. They exist because of them. If there is no problem, no struggle for the main character, there is, quite simply, no story. Can you imagine, for instance, *Shelter from the Wind*'s being told this way? *A girl went for a walk on the Oklahoma prairie, met an old woman and her dogs, and came home.* Boring! But even beyond being boring, it isn't a story at all, because there is no struggle.

So when I came to write *Shelter from the Wind*, I remembered both the thrill of the birth of Nimue's pups—and, in fact, the thrill I'd felt over the births of my own children—and the pain of that question I'd never had to face. I had, however, *felt* the question acutely. And because the feelings were there and the facts were there and because my story required an escalating problem, everything fell into place.

(I remember, though, that Peter, who was about ten at the time I was writing *Shelter from the Wind*, was furious with me for setting up the situation in which a puppy had to be killed. For a time, he even forbade me to use his dog in my story if I was going to have such a thing happen. Fortunately, after hearing a careful explanation of the necessity for conflict in stories, he finally relented, and I was able to complete my work as planned.)

Thus, my stories may make use of incidents from my own life. The story's foundation, however, must come from a place in me that's so deep that most of the time I'm not even thinking about it. I am probably writing to fill a hole, to satisfy a need left over from my own childhood. The main character, especially, and the main character's problem come out of that unfulfilled need of mine. Side characters are necessary to support or to be the occasion for the main character's struggle. I create them from fragments of the many, many people who have touched me, for good or ill, though no one I have ever known comes whole onto the page. And then I weave the plot out of more fragments, strongly felt moments, questions I have asked, unrealized desires of my own.

Mysterious? Hardly. Difficult? Sometimes. And yet at rare moments a story can leap into my brain and settle there like a cat choosing a lap. It has been a matter of learning to use what I feel, what I know, who I am. Of staying open to discovery. And of course, it has taken years of hard work to master the craft required to turn this strongly felt material into stories.

But first must come the feelings, being in touch with them, drawing energy from them. More than anything else, it is the fact of those feelings—and the strong urge to resolve them through stories—that makes me a writer.

5.

Imagination

I have taught fiction writing to adults—and sometimes to young writers—for over twenty years. In response to my students' struggles and to the questions they ask, I have developed some basic techniques for understanding the process of building stories. (My childhood background with my very logical father clearly put me in good stead here.) These elements of craft are spelled out in my book *What's Your Story? A Young Person's Guide to Writing Fiction.*

It was probably in addressing my students' needs, more than in the process of my own writing, that I developed a clear understanding of my craft. Much of what I do when I sit down to write is instinctive, and I suspect this is true for most professional writers. Or if it is not true in the early stages, it comes to be true as we move more deeply into our work.

But when that instinct fails—and it can fail me quite radically in the midst of some stories—I have found only one answer. That is to fall back on examining the elements of craft I spell out for my students. It is then that I am most grateful for my years of teaching, because what I have said again and again to my students can become, at that moment, the precise insight I need. *Oh,* I find myself exclaiming, *no wonder this character isn't believable! She is shifting direction too many times.* Or, *I can see why the energy of my story is slipping away. There is nothing left for my main character to want.*

But while craft is what I teach and what I emphasized in *What's Your Story?*, it is not, by any means, the whole picture. As important as it is, it is not even the most important part of the picture. It is simply the one part that can be clearly taught.

A writer who understands her craft can evaluate and revise her own stories. She can discover the places where instinct—or perhaps a better word is imagination—has failed. And then she can make her story work despite that failure. Or he can use his understanding of the basic shape of all stories to find the best form for a new one. But all the craft in the world won't make a *good* story if the writer doesn't approach the material with feeling and with imagination.

The first couple of times I taught a class in fiction writing, I pretty much said to my students, "Well . . . we're all here to write stories. So write!" And that is what many writing teachers seem to do. I discovered, however, that while some of my students began immediately and enthusiastically to write, others were utterly lost. They had no idea where to begin.

It was in response to those who didn't know where to begin, as well as to the constant need to define what was happening when my students got into difficulty with their stories, that I began asking myself questions. *What makes a story? How is a story different from a situation? How can I explain the difference? What does a writer need to know before beginning to write? What do I, myself, do to sustain tension from the beginning of a story to the end? What makes a character feel complex and "real"?* And on and on.

I have come to believe that this kind of understanding is essential, that it provides the solid underpinnings for creativity. And I have come to believe, too, that the best I can do for my students is to teach craft and encourage imagination.

Two elements of imagination are essential to writing stories. One is a sensitivity to language, a love for words, an appreciation for the sound of them, the shape of them on the tongue, an awareness of fine shades of meaning. The other is a sense of drama, a feeling for the impact of the story moment, an understanding of human desire. I have not learned how to teach either one. And yet I've never met a toddler just learning to speak, learning to appreciate stories, who didn't have both.

So perhaps the issue isn't that some of us are born with a "talent" that is withheld from others. Maybe some of us have merely unlearned what we once knew. Instead of rolling a word around on our tongues to relish its feel, we write it laboriously on a piece of paper and then look to see whether we have pleased the teacher. Instead of making up stories that will explain and empower our own lives, we sit in front of the television, waiting to be fed someone else's stories.

I've seen many mature adults who suffer, still, from a fear of the red pencil. They dread putting anything down on paper, fearful of having me, the teacher, see it, because they are certain they will be told that what they are doing is "wrong." Why wouldn't a love for language shrivel in the face of that kind of pressure? Learning to write under the threat of a red pencil is a bit like learning to play the piano knowing your hands will be whacked for every wrong note. Some people have taken piano lessons in that kind of atmosphere, I suppose, but I can't believe any of them have turned into great pianists . . . or even into people who play the piano in their homes with joy.

Most teachers today wield their red pencils more gently than did some teachers in the past. In writing classes there is far less emphasis on what is "wrong" and far more on self-expression, experimentation, and growth. Not that the rules—spelling and punctuation and grammar and all the elements of craft that make a good story—don't have to be learned. They do. But if the student doesn't begin with a desire to put words on paper, the rules are of little use.

Reading is one of the best ways I know to develop an awareness of and a love for words. Especially reading challenging, good material, material that is written with love and intended to elicit strong feelings from the reader. In no place is the love for language more distilled than in poetry. Too few people in our society read poetry, but a search for poems that speak to *you* can open new worlds.

Poems are especially exciting when they are read out

loud, so that one can savor the sound and the shape of the words on the tongue while sharing the writer's feelings. The popularity of rap is due to that same combination, with the listener taking pleasure in the sound of words that express the rapper's ideas and feelings.

The other element of imagination, a sense of drama, has origins that are no more mysterious. Stories, all stories, begin with desire . . . someone who wants something. And there must be a reason, a strong and important one, to keep the desire from being too easily satisfied. The main character will have to struggle to get what he wants . . . or perhaps to discover that he cannot get what he wants and to change his desire instead.

The challenge, then, isn't so much to figure out what the action of the story should be. (Curiously enough, though, when people ask where story ideas come from it is mostly the action they seem to be concerned about.) The primary challenge is to understand who the main character is. Why he wants what he does. Who stands in his way. What kind of struggle he is likely to engage in.

Where do we writers find the unfulfilled desire that sets our stories off? In no place more mysterious than ourselves, our own psyches, our own lives. How then can a writer's imagination be considered unusual, if we use nothing more unique than our own desires as the basis of our stories?

When the very idea of making up a story leaves a prospective writer feeling helpless, it is, I believe, because imagination is seen as strange and exotic. And yet the most concrete of thinkers not only is capable of imagining, but does so constantly. Someone worrying about what the neighborhood bully might do to him on the way home from school is using his imagination . . . and vividly. When we hear a strange sound in the middle of the night, we tumble into our own imaginings. Any time we look past the next day, or the next hill, we must employ imagination. If I think about a vacation I'm going to take, a person I'm going to meet, a goal I want to achieve, I'm using my imagination. And who doesn't do that?

Granted, I may live more deeply in my imagination than some others, just as some have a more instinctive feel for catching a ball than I. (In fact, almost anyone has a more instinctive feel for catching a ball than I do. The only thing I want to do when I see a ball coming toward me is get out of the way.)

Those who, for whatever reasons, have developed a fertile imagination, the kind that is perpetually leaping ahead, may discover stories more readily than others. But there is no one who doesn't *want* something. There is no one who hasn't dreamed that a particular desire will be fulfilled. And thus, there is no one who doesn't have, on this most basic level, the imagination required to write stories.

Let me demonstrate by turning to a story I wrote that may seem, on the surface, to be more imaginative than my others. It is the fantasy *Touch the Moon*. Since the story involves a china figurine that turns into a real horse—a talking horse, no less—it is very obviously the product of a fertile imagination. And yet it comes from my life in precisely the same way *Shelter from the Wind* does.

When I was a young girl, I wanted a horse, exactly as

Jennifer in the story wants a horse. I never asked my parents for one or even mentioned my desire, because I knew better. They wouldn't let me have the dog I kept begging for, so what chance did I have of getting a horse? I even knew exactly what they would have said if I'd asked: "We have no money to buy a horse, no place to keep a horse, and no one in our family knows enough about horses to take care of one properly." All those unsatisfactory adult reasons. But the impossibility of my desire didn't keep me from dreaming about horses.

Of course, I knew even less about horses than my parents did. They, at least, had both grown up on farms. The only opportunities I'd ever had to ride were when my family returned to my mother's childhood home in southeastern Minnesota. There on the farm was an elderly brown pony named Bobby.

About once during each summer visit, my cousins brought Bobby out of the barn, saddled him, helped me onto his back, and led the old pony slowly around the farmyard. Those few moments were always the highlight of my visit, though secretly I rather resented the tightly held reins. If only I'd had Bobby to myself, I knew we would have galloped freely across field and pasture.

The very last time I ever rode Bobby is the time I remember best. One of my cousins brought the old pony out of the barn, saddled him, and helped me onto his back. My cousin didn't immediately take the reins, however. Finding himself unencumbered and, no doubt, recognizing that his rider was not in control, Bobby took off in a sudden gallop, heading for the barn.

Well, I suppose I should have been thrilled, but the brief journey that followed was nothing like my dreams of galloping across field and pasture. In fact, it felt like nothing I'd ever wanted to do in my life. And though I tried quite desperately to hang on, within a very short distance I had tumbled off over Bobby's tail end . . . and that is just about my whole experience as a rider.

Except that I did another kind of riding, on another kind of trip my family took. My father's parents lived in California. So occasionally, instead of going to Minnesota for our vacation, we would take the long drive from Illinois to California and back again. On these trips, my brother and I always divided the back seat between us. The left side was his. The right side was mine. Nothing crossed the line in between.

Sitting on the right, I was always convinced that I had the better deal. My brother had nothing to look at all day long except approaching traffic. And I thought traffic was awfully boring stuff. From my side, though, I could watch the strip of grass running along the side of the road. Now, some people might think that watching a strip of grass is even more boring than watching traffic, but it depends entirely on what one does with it. And what I did with that strip of grass, in my mind, was to ride a beautiful palomino horse on it, right alongside the car.

It didn't matter how fast the car went, my horse and I kept up. When we came to a culvert, we jumped it. When we came to a fence, we jumped that. When the land was open and rolling, we would go racing across it and come running back to the car again. My horse and I never grew dusty or tired. My hair blew in the wind and never even got tangled. It was the most wonderful riding anyone could imagine, because it was, of course, imaginary riding.

So, years later, when I came to write *Touch the Moon*, I had two things in my mind and in my heart. One was those wonderful imaginary rides, all the way from Illinois to California and back again. The other was tumbling off over Bobby's tail end. And so I said to myself, *What if a girl who had dreamed about horses the way I used to, but who knew as little about them as I, suddenly had a horse? And what if she had no one to teach her to ride except the horse himself? And what if the horse wasn't especially cooperative? What would happen next?* And so my story was under way.

Of course, someone could say, reasonably enough, "But you have always had an active imagination. Look at the way you spent your time in the car." And that is certainly true. I am convinced, though, that we all have similar experiences if we only become aware of them.

Notice that *Touch the Moon* isn't based on the *facts* of my own life. It isn't the story of a girl sitting in a car and dreaming of riding. I used the *feelings* connected with those facts, and there I found the energy for my story.

When we writers, young or old, feel that our imaginations are inadequate, it is usually for one of two reasons. Either we are trying to stay too close to the circumstances of our own lives, or we are trying to take off from a point that has no connection with our own experience and feelings.

If the only stories I could write were ones that had actually happened to me, my career would have been over before it had begun. And if I had to produce stories about anything I couldn't feel, I would be equally stymied. The secret is that I begin with a foundation of my own feelings and then move out from there. A story about spider people taking over the world might be just right for someone who has always abhorred—or been fascinated by—bugs. One about a boy falling in love could come alive for a writer waiting impatiently for his first romance . . . or remembering one from long ago.

Everyone has an imagination. It is the *what if* of our daily lives. The reason that imagination is so difficult to teach in a class—or in a book, for that matter—is that it is so personal, so unique.

As are our stories.

6.

Moving Beyond Experience

From the time I began going into schools as an author to talk to kids about my early books, I was asked the question:

"When are you going to write a book about a boy?"

"I don't know if I ever will," I used to reply. "Obviously, I was a girl. I know how it feels to be a girl. I don't know if I could do a good job of writing about a boy."

But the next time I was in a school, the question would come up again. "When are you going to write a book about a boy?"

Finally I had to try it. There would be, I decided, a boy named Steve at the center of *Rain of Fire*. The whole idea felt like a stretch for me. I hadn't even been a tomboy when I was a kid; how could I feel my way inside the skin of a male character? Because I needed a familiar take-off point, I decided to surround Steve with as many externals from my own life as possible. That is why *Rain of Fire* is the only one of my stories set in the time of my childhood—just after World War II—and the only one of my books to make use of my own childhood environment—the mill housing I grew up in. Those were the externals that were going to make Steve come to life.

I wrote the first draft, and by the time I was through, I was quite fond of Steve. *Who wouldn't be?* I said to myself. *After all, he's a nice kid.* Then I gave the manuscript to a friend to read and waited for her response. (This is something I do at different points as I'm working, because every writer needs the objectivity only an outside perspective can bring. The most important outside perspective comes from my editor, of course, but I use other readers in the early stages. This way I can take care of as many issues as possible before my editor ever sees the manuscript.)

I have been writing nearly all my life, and I've had lots of helpful comments from different people at different stages of my work, most of which I no longer remember. However, the words of the friend who read the first draft of *Rain of Fire* are still etched in my brain. As she handed the manuscript back to me, she said, "Marion, by the end of the story, I like Celestino better than I like Steve." Which was bad news. Steve is the story's hero, and Celestino is the villain.

How can you prefer Celestino? I shouted inside my head after my friend had gone. (I do all my shouting inside my head instead of at my editors or readers. Otherwise, I'd run out of people willing to comment on my writing.) *That's really dumb! Didn't you notice what a nice kid Steve is?*

Then I sat down and read the novel again, keeping her comment in mind. To my dismay, I discovered that she was right. Being a "nice kid" wasn't enough to make Steve an appealing character. And all the externals with which I had surrounded him—the time of my own childhood, the place of my growing up—had done little or nothing to make him come alive.

That's it, I said, still to myself. *It's perfectly clear that I can't write about boys, or at least not about a boy from the inside. I shouldn't have tried.*

But I *had* tried. The story was written, at least a first draft. And when I speak of a first draft, I am actually talking about months of writing and rewriting and rewriting and rewriting just to make my way from beginning to end. I had at least six months invested in Steve and his story already. So I wasn't exactly thrilled with the idea of throwing out the stack of pages and turning to something else. And on top of that, before I'd written *Rain of Fire* I'd written another story—this one with a girl at the center—that had simply failed to work. In fact, my editor had turned it down, which is something that had never happened before. If I gave up on Steve, I'd be proving to myself that I had run out of stories to tell.

At the time, because I had been feeling finished with *Rain of Fire*—I always feel finished at the end of a first draft, but I never am—I had already been gathering ideas for another story. This one—sigh of relief—would be about a girl. And the one thing I knew about this girl was that she would be a liar.

She wouldn't be a vicious liar. She wouldn't, in fact, intend anything bad with her lies at all. But she would be the kind of kid for whom the truth simply isn't good enough to cover some situations, and her lies would pop out before she knew what she was going to say.

Where did this idea for the main character of my next story come from? Simple. From inside me.

When I was a kid, I really was quite truthful about what I said. In fact, about the only time I ever lied was when I put words on paper. If a teacher asked for a theme on a subject such as "My Summer Vacation," my intentions were always good. But even if my summer vacation had seemed interesting at the time, once I began to write about it, the whole thing instantly turned boring.

So . . . we drove to California to visit my grandparents. How do you write about that? We drove all day. We ate bologna sandwiches. My brother and I squabbled a bit in the back seat. We played the alphabet game. (The winner was the first person who got all the letters of the alphabet—in order, of course—off the billboards and signs on his side of the road.) We read the Burma Shave signs, a series of small red-and-white signs that marched alongside the road, giving advice in verse and proclaiming the virtues of Burma Shave shaving cream. We kept track of license plates from different states. I daydreamed.

At night we camped. My parents set up their tent and the army-surplus jungle hammocks my brother and I used, then we all had supper, went to sleep, got up in the morning, broke camp, and climbed back into the car. Who wanted to hear about any of that?

I would begin to write, but then I'd stop. *Wouldn't it have been interesting,* I'd find myself thinking, my pencil poised in the air, *if a bear had wandered through our campsite while we slept?* And then I'd remind myself, *Well, a bear* could *have come through our campsite while we slept.* And the next thing I knew I would find myself writing that an enraged bear had, in fact, charged into our campsite. He was big, ferocious, and maybe even rabid, and he'd torn open my parents' tent with one swipe of his razor-sharp claws. Even my father, brave as he was, hadn't known what to do, so it had been a good thing I'd been there to save the day. Picking up a log still smoldering from the fire, I set the beast's tail aflame and sent him howling back into the woods. After which we all went back to sleep.

I don't know how my teachers felt about my family's exciting summer vacations, but none of them ever complained. Of course, they hadn't been there. How could they know if a bear had wandered into our campsite or not? And besides, I wrote reasonably well, which is what concerned them most.

The problem came, however, when it was time to take the papers home. My parents, I knew, were not going to say, "Marion, what a fine imagination you have!" They were going to say, "Marion, why are you writing all those lies?" I couldn't have said why I was writing lies, except that they were so much more interesting than the truth. And I knew full well that my parents wouldn't be impressed with an answer like that.

I solved my problem pretty easily. My house was a good mile from the school, and during the walk home, I passed several large, military-green containers painted with the words KEEP YOUR CITY CLEAN. Being a good citizen, I kept my city *very* clean. I tore up the offending papers and tucked them into the very bottom of those cans so they couldn't possibly be resurrected, and my family never knew what fascinating adventures we'd had on our summer vacations.

I did some of the same kind of verbal embroidery when I wrote letters or in the diary I occasionally kept. But my intention was never to deceive. In fact, I always started out meaning to tell the truth. I did. But I couldn't seem to stop the truth from turning into a good story along the way.

So years later, there I was, thinking of writing a story about a girl who lied . . . and there I was, faced with Steve in *Rain of Fire*, a nice kid who just wasn't making it as a main character. And that was when I discovered why he didn't work. Because Steve was a boy, I had given him nothing from my own insides. As though a boy's insides would be so radically different from my own that I couldn't use anything of my own inner experience. But maybe—it finally occurred to me—just maybe it was possible that I did know something about Steve from the inside. Maybe he was a liar.

Following my own childhood experience, Steve lied, but not because he didn't care about the truth. He didn't even intend, actually, to lie. The lies just seemed to pop out because the truth wasn't good enough for some of the situations Steve found himself in.

And so I returned to *Rain of Fire*, and for the first time, my main character began to come alive. By the time my work was done, he had all the complexity of one of my female protagonists because I had invested him with a chunk of my own feelings.

If you read *Rain of Fire*, you will see that I didn't simply go back to the manuscript and stick in a lie or two. The novel was entirely reconceived. In the final version it is Steve's lies that make the story happen from the beginning. And because of this, I hope—and from my readers' responses I think I can believe—Steve comes to life.

I went on after *Rain of Fire* to write other novels with a boy at the center: *On My Honor, Face to Face, A Question of Trust*. Even Purrloom Popcorn, the cat in *Ghost Eye*, is male. I am able to do that now because I have learned that feelings have no gender. In order to write about a boy, I have to understand some basic facts about male culture, of course. Exactly the way I have to understand about other kinds of differences in the surface lives of my characters. But I grew up with a father and a brother. I was married for nearly thirty years. I have a son and have had foster sons, as well. I have friends and students who are male. I have had lifelong contact with maleness.

These days few reader responses delight me more than the occasional one I get from a boy who has read one of my books and is surprised, afterward, to discover that I am a woman. (The spelling of my name hides my gender, since Marion can also be a man's name.) That response lets me know, again, that my discovery is valid.

A librarian once told me that she had recommended *Face to Face* to a boy who usually disliked reading but loved anything about whitewater rafting. "When he brought it back," she said, "he didn't comment on the excitement of the rafting scenes, though I'm sure he found them exciting. He said instead, 'That author understands me.'"

If I do, it's only because I have worked to understand *myself* and then used what I have come to know to create believable characters, male and female. And that kind of understanding is open to every one of us.

It is in knowing myself, really knowing myself, that I can know others. And it is in knowing myself and others that I can write stories, even stories about people who are different in important ways from me.

7.

From Your Story to Mine . . . Plagiarism?

When people are just beginning to write fiction, they are often unduly concerned about plagiarism. They are afraid either that they will borrow from someone else's work without meaning to or that another writer, perhaps less innocently, will copy theirs. But I have found that plagiarism is rarely an issue. If a writer writes out of deep personal feelings, plagiarism cannot happen.

We all have strong feelings attached to singular moments in our lives: the death of a pet, falling in love, making a goal in the last seconds of a game. But equally important feelings come out of the texture of our daily lives: our relationships with parents and siblings, the satisfaction of learning how to skate, fear of the dark. And there are times, even, when those feelings are very much attached to stories others have told us. Any of these experiences can be the source of energy for a new story, but if we begin writing from a core of our own feelings, the story we write will, almost inevitably, be ours, too.

People often ask me if I ever get ideas from stories I have read, and yes, I do. Fiction is referred to as an "imitation of life," but the truth is that stories are, even more, an imitation of other stories. The first business of anyone who wants to write is to read widely and deeply. For it is only in discovering what others have done that we learn how to begin to attempt to do it ourselves.

Of course, if an idea of mine begins with a moment that has struck me in another writer's story, I will not sit down and start to write until the idea has become fully mine. I read novels constantly, both those written for young people and those for adults. I read so much, in fact, that I sometimes feel that for every new book I read, two earlier ones tumble out of my brain and are lost. And this mass of reading inevitably forms part of who I am, what I think, what I know.

I discovered the inescapable connection between my reading and my own writing with the publication of my first novel, *Shelter from the Wind*. Shortly after it came out, a woman who was probably fifteen years older than I said, "You know, I was reminded of another book when I read *Shelter from the Wind*, but you're probably too young to have even heard of it."

"What's it called?" I asked politely, not expecting any great revelations. I hadn't, after all, been thinking of any other book when I was writing.

And she replied, "*Understood Betsy* by Dorothy Canfield Fisher."

I was speechless, because I knew instantly that she was right to think of *Understood Betsy* when she was reading my book. I had read it as a child, and though I hadn't thought of the story for many years, it did, indeed, influence my writing of *Shelter from the Wind*.

Because the library in my small town was limited and my parents rarely bought contemporary children's books for my brother and me, I grew up reading my mother's childhood books. So the stories that had affected my childhood were, for the most part, a generation older than I. And in fact, not only had I read *Understood Betsy*, but that story had had a particularly strong impact on me as a child.

Understood Betsy is the story of a girl who is being reared with much care and caution by two maiden aunts. One of the aunts develops tuberculosis, and the doctor insists that Betsy be sent to live elsewhere to keep her safe from infection. She goes to stay with some cousins on a farm. The cousins are casual in their treatment of her and almost, it seemed to me—who was something of an understood Betsy myself—cruel. They expect Betsy to do for herself in all kinds of ways that her aunts had previously done for her. They even expect her to work in the house and on the farm. But they also surround her with a very physical love.

At first resentful, Betsy gradually comes to thrive under the cousins' casual but very solid caring. And when she is given a chance to return to her aunts at the end of the story, she decides to remain where she is. (The aunt who had been ill met and fell in love with a man at the sanatorium, so she is about to embark on a new life, and Betsy's decision brings mutual relief.)

I knew when I read the book that Betsy had made the right decision, but still I couldn't overcome my amazement. The idea that it might be good for a child to have to take care of herself in some ways was almost beyond my comprehension. But I took it in as I read. In fact, I *felt* Betsy's change, almost as though it had happened in my own life. And I remembered her story years later, as an adult, when I didn't even realize I was remembering.

Thus, when I wrote *Shelter from the Wind*, I discovered again, this time with Stacy, that sometimes the pride of doing for oneself is more healing than any amount of being cared for.

Does what I carried from Ms. Fisher's book to mine amount to plagiarism? No, because the story passed through me, through my life and experience, in a way that made it wholly mine. You could read the two books side by side and not find a single sentence repeated, not find one character like any other. The two are so different, actually, that unless you were considering only their underlying themes, you probably wouldn't notice any connection between them at all. But my novel grew, in an important way, out of the other.

They share, not because I borrowed the theme of *Shelter from the Wind* from a book I had read as a child, but because the book I had read when I was young touched me, even transformed me. It made me understand something important about myself and the nature of life. And that kind of understanding creates energy, even years later.

For those who have no interest in writing, in making stories, such a discovery could probably be used in other ways. Perhaps by helping one's own children learn independence. Maybe by becoming a banker devoted to helping small businesses thrive. Because I am a fiction writer, I took the discovery I made in that story and turned it into another story.

Another of my stories begins with another book from

my childhood, this one consciously remembered. I no longer recall the title, but the magic of the story stays with me still. The entire novel occurred in a child's playhouse. It was a full-sized structure, big enough for the little girl who was the main character to walk into, and it had been built for her by her father. At the opening of the story, the father has completed the work on the playhouse and is planting a small pine tree on each side of the front door. He and his daughter name the playhouse Twin Pines.

From there, the story turns magical. Any time the girl is away from the playhouse, her dolls, now residing in it, come alive and have all sorts of adventures. The dolls' adventures intrigued me, but they are not what I remember from that long-ago story. In fact, I can't recall any of the specifics of those adventures at all.

What was important for me, what was astonishing and truly magical, wasn't that the dolls came alive when their owner wasn't there. My dolls did *that*. In my imagination I had invested them with such life that I never ceased to expect to come into my room and find them walking around and carrying on conversations with one another. What caught my attention, rather, was the idea that there might be a father anywhere in the world who would build a beautiful, big, expensive playhouse just for his little girl. That was the thought I came back to again and again. Could there be such a father? Really? Could there ever have been such a lucky little girl?

The whole concept seemed far more fantastic to me than the prospect of dolls' coming to life, and I puzzled over it deeply. I am the owner of a spacious town home today, but there is a part of me that still longs for a play-house like the one in that book. Even more important, it longs for a father who could have understood and acknowledged that desire.

Recently, one of my editors, Dianne Hess, and I were discussing the next book I would do for her. She wanted me to consider writing a British-style fantasy. Her love of such books was a compelling call from her own childhood and, in fact, was the lure that drew her into working with children's books in the first place. My initial reaction to her suggestion, however, was negative.

I had, of course, read and even loved the *Chronicles of Narnia* by C.S. Lewis and other such fantasies as she had in mind, but I was certain my style wouldn't accommodate anything like that. Still, the conversation moved on to my memory of the book about the child's playhouse . . . and the father who had built it. Dianne recognized and responded to the energy she had tapped, and as often happens, her response brought more of my energy to the surface. By the time we were through talking, another playhouse—and a very different father—were beginning to find their shape.

Without hearing this explanation, no one would make any kind of connection between that original book, should they know it, and the story I am working on now. The two are very different.

My story, as I am discovering it, reaches beyond my old longing for a playhouse (or even for a father who might build such a haven for his little girl). It explores another childhood fantasy of mine, the ability to move inside a picture on a wall and to become part of the world of that picture. So the playhouse in my story serves an entirely different function than it did in the story I so loved as a child. Instead of providing a setting for dolls' adventures, it becomes a door into another world.

Thus, though my story grew quite directly out of another, it became something entirely different along the way. That is because my idea came not so much from the plot of the original book as from the feelings that plot engendered in me. And as I began to build my story, inevitably I gathered other feelings, other experiences, other questions and convictions of my own to flesh out the story I wanted to tell. Perhaps my story will then give energy to other people's lives and stories.

This is not plagiarism. It's not even borrowing. It's simply a matter of passing the riches on.

8.

Truth and Reality

"*B*ut did it really happen?"

After "Where do your story ideas come from?" this seems to be the question authors, at least authors of realistic fiction, are most often asked. And of all my books, *On My Honor* is the one about which the question comes up most insistently.

When I am asked about that book, I sometimes find myself reluctant to reply unless I have a chance to talk about the way I use real life in my other stories as well. Ultimately, I worked the same way with *On My Honor* as I have with all my other novels, but on the surface the manner in which I came by the story seems very different.

So here comes the confession, and the explanation: *On My Honor* is, from beginning to end, based on a real event. It is the only one of my books that is. Joel's story isn't something that happened to me. Rather, it is something that happened to a friend of mine when we were both in our early teens.

My friend and another boy whom I didn't know went down to the Vermillion River to swim. (Those who have read the book will recognize that I used the same setting for the story as the one in which the real event occurred. It was, after all, *my* setting, too.) We were all forbidden to swim in the river because it was dirty and dangerous, but for whatever reason—perhaps it was simply a hot day—the boys decided to go in.

The other boy, the one I didn't know, wasn't a good swimmer. Or perhaps he couldn't swim at all. I'm not sure. Part of what makes rivers dangerous is that the movement of the water alters the bottom constantly, so it is never possible to predict what the depth of a certain spot will be. At some point, it seems, the other boy stepped off, quite unexpectedly, into deep water and went under.

When my friend saw that his companion had disappeared, he tried repeatedly to dive for him. He searched and searched. But the water was murky and the current was swift, and he finally had to give up. Knowing that his friend had drowned, he apparently felt so frightened—and so guilty—that he went home, went upstairs to his room, closed the door, and didn't tell anyone what had happened.

Eventually, the other boy's family reported him missing, and the police were called. After a sequence of events I know nothing about, the surviving boy finally relented, telling the adults what had happened. The river was dragged, and the body was found.

My friend never talked to me about that day. I can well imagine that he must not have felt like talking about it to anyone. But I can still remember where I was standing in my yard when one of his younger brothers told me about the drowning. And I can remember feeling, in my very core, what it must have been like to climb out of that river, knowing that nothing could ever erase the terrible consequences of the moments that had just passed.

I didn't feel my friend's plight because anything similar had ever happened to me. Nothing had. I had never been involved in an incident in which anyone died. I had never been involved in an incident in which anyone was hurt seriously enough to matter. I had never even gone swimming in the Vermillion River. I was a pretty good kid. (Actually, I was something of a wimp of a kid. If I was told not to swim in the river, I didn't swim in the river.)

But I don't suppose there is anyone alive, certainly not anyone old enough to read this, who hasn't at some time wished it were possible to undo a painful mistake. I know I have. There was the time, for instance, when I overheard a teacher whom I very much admired talking to another teacher. I thought I heard her say that her husband, who worked for the railroad, had been "drunk." What she actually said was that he had been "bumped," meaning temporarily laid off. But I repeated the story as I thought I had heard it, and by the time I learned my mistake, my teacher was angry with me and I was in an agony of shame. *If only,* I thought, *I could go back and live that day over! I'd never say such a thing.* We all come to understand, however, that there will be no opportunity to live days over.

Thus on that bright summer day, I stood in the green safety of my own yard and, for just a moment, *felt* what had happened to a boy with whom I had grown up. I never heard anything more about the event. My parents didn't discuss it in front of me. No one in my friend's family ever spoke of it to me again, either. And what details I had were very sketchy. I didn't even know what led him to reveal the truth. Or what the adults had done when he had. I knew only that my friend had not been punished, that his father had said, "You've already been punished enough."

I probably forgot about the tragedy quite soon. After all, it hadn't happened to me. It wasn't until many years later that the events of that day slipped back into my mind, and I began to think of them as the basis for a story. My first reaction was reluctance. I had never used anything so whole, let alone an event which must have been so traumatic in the life of someone I knew. And I was acutely aware that I stood entirely outside of all that had happened. I couldn't, for an instant, *know* what it had been like to be in the river that day. In fact, it was possible that even my memory of what I had been told might no longer be accurate since it had never been reinforced by further discussion. Still, the idea wouldn't go away.

I drew on the event first to write a short story. Because I didn't feel there was enough space or time in a short story to deal with the trauma of death, I made the drowning a fake one. An older boy compels a younger one to come into a forbidden river by pretending that he is drowning. In going into the river to rescue the older boy, the younger one not only sets himself up to be ridiculed, but comes close to drowning himself. That story was written on request for a magazine, and when the editor who had asked for it turned it down—apparently finding the material too strong—I put the manuscript away.

The original idea—the facts, as I knew them—remained, however. And I discovered that I was beginning to carry around in my head the boy whose companion had drowned. It wasn't my friend I was thinking about. The boy I carried was my own internalization of my friend and his long-ago plight. Joel, an entirely different boy, constructed out of my own strong feelings surrounding such an imagined situation, began to come to life. And I wrote the novel.

When I report this background to adults or to young people, I always suspect that their unspoken response is, "Well, that one was easy. You just took what happened and wrote it down. It's almost like you stole the story."

And yet, *On My Honor* grew in exactly the same way each of my other stories grows, even those stories which begin from a base of far fewer facts. I moved into my main character, and I began to ask myself questions: *Who is he? What does he want? Who is Tony, and why are Joel and Tony friends?* The two, as I conceived them, were so different. *What will it be like for Joel when he has to face the fact that Tony has drowned? When he has to face Tony's parents, the police, his own father?*

The real event as it happened to my friend gave me answers to none of these questions . . . except that I knew Joel would, at first, try to hide what had happened, and I knew his father wouldn't punish him. Those two points from the actual event felt right to me. They fit the character I was building in my head.

A close reading of *On My Honor* that takes into

account what I knew of the real circumstances will easily demonstrate how much of the story comes from my imagination, how little from the hard facts. From the first line, when Joel is reacting to Tony's challenge to climb the dangerous bluffs in Starved Rock State Park, the story is mine, not my childhood friend's. In fact, I made it a point to change Joel's family to make it entirely unlike the original boy's. I wanted those few people who would recognize the real incident—especially my friend from the past—to understand that I was not writing his story. I was only borrowing some of its surfaces in order to write my own.

All of the details of the relationships between the boys and their families, all of the details of the drowning, all of Joel's actions before and afterward were created out of my imagination. I knew none of this from the real event. I didn't even know why the boys had chosen to go swimming or anything about the one who had drowned, not even his name. Most significant of all, I knew absolutely nothing of what my friend had thought and felt on that day. And yet at every moment in *On My Honor* a reader knows exactly what Joel is thinking and feeling. Where did all of that come from? From the same place it does in the writing of each of my stories . . . from inside me.

When I write a story, I usually begin with a moment in reality. I begin with something I have read in the newspaper or experienced in my own life or heard someone tell. And I carry it with me, feeling it, thinking about it, letting it grow, until it ripens into a story. When the opening words are singing in my brain, when I can feel the story's resolution, when I can sense the story's connection to my own life, I sit down and begin to write.

I wrote the first draft of *On My Honor* in two weeks. I haven't written any other novel so fast, either before or since. It was almost as if the story lived in the tips of my fingers and simply flowed out when I sat down at the keyboard. The subsequent drafts, fine-tuning the story and making it work, took most of six months.

There remains for me, however, an important difference between *On My Honor* and all my other books. In none of my other novels would anyone I know—or anyone I don't know, for that matter—have reason to feel that I had borrowed my story from his or her life.

I did borrow the surfaces of my story from my friend's terrible experience, as I said before, and I have often wished that I had found ways to change it more substantively so that the borrowing wouldn't have been so apparent. At the very least, I could have changed the location, I suppose, but when I was writing, such a change didn't seem possible. I had spent a great deal of time on the banks of the Vermillion River. And I knew, without ever having experienced it myself, what the tug of its current would be like.

When *On My Honor* was first published, I wrote my childhood friend, whom I hadn't seen since we were both grown, to explain my borrowing. I wanted him to know how respectfully I had used that piece of his boyhood. I wanted him to know, too, that I didn't think for a moment that I was writing *his* story. It couldn't be his. It could only be my own. Because my story is the only one I know well enough to tell.

I wish I could conclude this account by saying that he

wrote back, forgiving my intrusion into his life, perhaps even telling me that he had found the reliving of those terrible events to be healing in some way. The truth is that he never answered my letter. I heard through his family that he found the book painful to read, that he would read a few pages and put it down, pick it up later to read again and once more put it down. I don't know if he was ever able to read it to the end, nor do I know if he resented my having borrowed from this tragedy of his boyhood. I only know that the story I wrote has a life of its own, quite apart from my memories or his pain, which I hope justifies, at least in part, the choices I made.

ia

It is inevitable, I suppose, that readers will want to ask, "Did it really happen?" And while I understand their curiosity, the question always seems irrelevant to me. It doesn't matter what part of a story comes from actual events. It matters whether a story is *true*. And truth in fiction comes, not from external events—did they occur in that manner or did they not?—but from the deepest understandings of the heart.

On many occasions when I have been visiting different communities across the country, someone will say, speaking of *On My Honor*, "You know, we had something just like that happen here." And they will go on to tell of a drowning or other accident in which the child who was left behind was so frightened and felt so guilty that for hours, or perhaps for days, he or she told no one what had happened. I have come to realize that the circumstances of the story are universal. I could have gotten my original idea from any one of these tellings or from newspaper accounts of similar events that had happened to children I had never met . . . or even strictly from my own imagination.

But it doesn't matter, ultimately, where the idea originated. What makes the story work, if it works, are my own strong feelings . . . and my ability to make the reader feel, too.

On My Honor began with my friend's ordeal. It passed through my own psyche to gather richness, depth, authenticity. And it became something larger and truer than either his experience or mine. It became a story.

9.

Creativity

When Sir Isaac Newton, the English philosopher and mathematician who formulated the law of gravity, was asked how he came up with his unique insights, he replied, "By keeping the idea always before my mind." I believe that statement explains much of what people refer to as creativity. It isn't that creative people—if some of us can be considered creative and others not, which I doubt—think differently than others. If there is any difference at all, it is that some of us hang onto an idea more persistently, more obsessively, than others.

Most writers' early stories are not very successful, and the lack of success often goes beyond issues of craft yet to be learned to the story conception itself. The story idea is simply not "creative" enough. Which means that the writer hasn't hung on to it long enough, hasn't thought about it persistently enough, hasn't given it the time and attention that will allow it to ripen into a story ready to be written.

Everyone knows our brains are supposed to look rather like a mass of large, gray spaghetti. But in my imagination, my brain doesn't look like gray spaghetti at all. In fact, when I think of the inside of my skull, I see neat shelves lined up along the back of it. And a great deal of my time is spent rummaging among the contents of those shelves.

Moving through my days, I do all the ordinary things everyone else does. I eat breakfast. I read the newspaper. I talk to friends. I walk the dog. I read or occasionally watch television or a movie. I go camping. I paddle my kayak around a lake or go snowshoeing through the winter woods. And, of course, I write. I spend anywhere from four to six hours a day on my current project (and then two or three more on correspondence and other more mechanical kinds of writing).

Anyone watching me might say that I spend four to six hours a day being "creative." But in actual fact, my writing time involves only one part of my creativity, and not necessarily the most important part. It is often when I am walking the dog . . . or chopping onions . . . or talking to my partner that my most creative work is done. And it all has to do with those shelves.

The creative work for one of my stories begins with an idea that catches my attention. At first, the idea is simply what was given me, something I read or heard or saw, an incident with feelings attached but no particular meaning. And because the feelings attached to the idea seem important—I may not understand why they seem important to me, only that they do—I pick it up and put it on one of my back-of-the-brain shelves.

One of those shelves holds an image of one of my cats from a small incident that happened one day. I walked into the kitchen and found Popcorn, our white

Cornish rex, sitting in the middle of the table. I was about to shoo her off, but Ann, my partner, held up her hand. "Wait," she said. "Look what she's doing." So I stopped to look. It was snowing outside, the first snow of the season, and Popcorn was staring intently out of the kitchen window, obviously fascinated by the falling flakes. After another moment of intense scrutiny, she turned to look through the pass-through into the dining room and through the dining room's deck doors at the snow falling on that side of our town home as well. Then she looked up at the ceiling. It couldn't have been more clear that she was trying to figure out why, if those interesting things were coming down in front of the house and in back of the house, too, nothing was falling on her.

Popcorn has provided the kernel of an idea for two of my novels, *Ghost Eye* and *A Question of Trust*. But I haven't yet found a story out of her confusion over snow. Perhaps I never will, but I have always been fascinated by anything which demonstrates an animal's mind at work, so that example stays on the shelf. Maybe I'll write a picture book someday about a housebound cat in love with the outside world, with its snow, rain, wind, and trees. In fact, I even have a title in mind for such a book, *The Cat Who Loved a Tree*. (Popcorn falls madly in love with our Christmas tree every year, too.) Until then the idea remains on its shelf, and I take it down to consider it from time to time.

As a child, I often daydreamed about flying. Not just the physical act of leaving the ground and gliding through the air, though that was important, of course.

But about the wings I would have. I knew exactly what they would be like. They were angel wings, large and white and feathered. And they not only permitted me to fly, but they were the object of great admiration. In my imaginings, I preened and combed and cared for those wings. I even had thin rubber covers to pull over them to keep the feathers dry when I swam in the community pool. So it isn't surprising that a girl with wings is an idea on one of my shelves.

Actually, I have used part of that idea for an easy reader, *Alison's Wings*, but only part. The rest stays behind, waiting to find the right story.

I used to daydream, as well, about having a tail. I considered different kinds. The curled tail of a husky. The more slender and smoothly furred tails of my cats. Even a skinny mouse tail would have been better, I thought, than no tail at all. I spent time wondering whether a tail might be thought a shameful abnormality (by those who failed to understand how fine tails were). If I had one, I knew I would carry it proudly. I would even have holes cut in all my clothes so it could show.

But the tail I longed for most passionately was the prehensile tail of a monkey. I wanted a tail I could hang from, even swing by. One that I could snake over my shoulder or past my waist and use like an extra hand. How sad it is to have been born without so wonderful an appendage!

That idea, too, remains on a shelf.

One morning several years ago my local newspaper carried a story about an abduction. In a small town in Minnesota a man had stepped out of a stand of trees and taken a young boy at gunpoint, sending his brother and the friend who was with him away. As I read, I found myself *feeling* the boy's plight—and his family's—as everyone else who read the story surely did. That event, too, went on the shelf, along with all my strong feelings about it.

I am making the entire process sound very simple, I know, but the fact is . . . it *is* simple. Perhaps I'm giving away secrets, demystifying what some might prefer to keep shrouded and dark. But there is actually little mystery in the activity of gathering ideas. And yet this gathering lies at the heart of creativity.

If there is a secret to creativity, it lies in what we writers do with the contents of those shelves.

Too many people attempt to gather an idea and to write it all at the same time, which is rather like gobbling a dinner of green apples. You're apt to get indigestion before you're done. Ideas must ripen before they are of much use. Contrary to apples, however, they aren't likely to ripen well unless they are handled, turned over, considered again and again.

If I am different from some others, that difference is not that I am more creative, but simply that I keep "the idea always before my mind." How do I do that? Through a very conscious determination. Through an obsession, even. The stories I write must be so important to me that they begin to take over my thoughts.

I have trained myself, any time I am doing something that doesn't require my full concentration, to return again and again and again to those shelves. I take an idea down, turn it over, examine it, and put it back again. I take down another idea and "try it on for size." Or if I am working consciously on a particular story, as I often am, I go immediately to the shelf that story idea is on, pick it up, weigh it, ask myself questions about it, let it slip from my hand. I allow my mind to drift, checking out the contents of other shelves, planning a grocery list, remembering tasks that must be done, but only briefly. After a minute or two, I return, very intentionally, to that same story shelf again. And again. And again . . .

It's a process that has a great deal in common with rolling a large snowball. As I turn an idea over in my mind, time after time, something new sticks to it. Sometimes some of the things that stuck earlier fall off. *No, that isn't going to work.* But little by little, the idea grows. New thoughts don't come every time I handle an idea, but if the idea is a good one for me, they do come, gradually and steadily. And in fact, I have a very simple way of telling when an idea is a fit. My excitement over it builds. The idea stretches and grows. It challenges me deeply.

A hundred times a day, a thousand even, I return to my current story idea. The ripening story becomes so much a part of me that it is never very far from my conscious thoughts. Other less urgent ideas will fall off their shelves from time to time, too. And as each one presents itself, I give it a moment's attention, then return to the one that feels most urgent to me.

I have found it essential, though, for the idea I am working on to be held lightly. The moment I panic, the moment I try to force my brain-shelf to yield up its riches so I can get this blasted thing moving, a door I didn't even know was there slams shut. And then my doubting self moves in to turn the key in the lock.

Who do you think you are, she demands to know, *trying to write this story? You don't know enough about this subject even to begin. Besides, you can't really write anyway. And if you do manage to get the words down, it's going to be too much like something you've done before or, even worse, like something someone better than you has already written.*

And she goes on and on, yammering and berating very much in my own voice, but somehow with an uncanny authority. (It is curious how believable I can be when I criticize myself, how unconvincing when I give myself praise.)

The most effective way I've found to turn off my doubting self is to pretend I don't care, to pretend what I'm doing isn't all that crucial anyway. I'm just playing, after all. *So, I've looked at this particular story idea 342 times already today. Isn't it fun? Maybe I'll even write it down when I'm ready. Maybe I won't. But now all I'm doing is thinking, and there's no law against that, is there?* If I don't squeeze the thought too hard or get it slammed in the door, maybe it will survive to become a story.

A good idea, one that truly belongs to me, will grow and change gradually, day after day. Sometimes the idea I began with will disappear along the way, and another thought, one the first idea led to, now stands solidly at the core of my story. An example of this is the idea I mentioned earlier which was drawn from a newspaper story about an abduction.

For years I planned to write a story about a boy who was abducted. I carried the idea around with me, took it out to examine day after day. And gradually it did grow, but the growth was slow, even painful. Then an article appeared in my local paper about the family whose son and brother had been torn so terribly from their lives. Three years had passed. For all the family's continuing efforts and the help of many others, there was still no information about what had happened to the boy, whether he might be dead or alive. As I read that new story, I understood for the first time exactly what was wrong with the idea I was trying to develop.

I discovered that my deepest attention had never really centered on the boy who was lost or on the details of what might have happened to him. My mind didn't fly after him, wondering what his days and nights might have been like in the hands of the abductor and how he must have felt to be chosen in so terrible a way. I was far more interested, I finally understood, in the brother who had been left behind. How had the abduction affected him? And the curious thing I realized then was that the remaining brother had always been the focus of my attention, the source of my energy when I thought about this potential story. The other material was so much more obvious, though, so much more dramatic, that I hadn't noticed where my own real interest lay.

I haven't written that story yet, but I will. It still needs more shelf time before it's ready. And by the time it finds its way to the page, it will be quite distinct from the original story that set me thinking about abduction. It will probably be unrecognizable, in fact. But for whatever reason, the idea of survivor guilt moves me. That is obvious from *On My Honor* and *Rain of Fire*. And so the same energy that gave me those stories will eventually give me this one as well.

It doesn't matter, finally, where the idea began. When I have examined it, felt it, added to it, and let other ideas fall away again thousands and thousands of times, it will finally be mine.

A writer's unique creativity? Yes, I suppose. And yet it is a creativity that is accessible to anyone. At least it is accessible to anyone who cares passionately enough about stories to want to spend a lifetime considering them, sorting them, growing them. That is the secret, really.

Creativity lies in caring enough about a single thing to hang on to it, to hold it up, to think about it, to obsess about it. In my years of teaching, I have known many students who are as talented as I, if talent is measured in an ability to use language, in a sense of drama. It is more rare that I find students whose need to do this thing, whose obsession with it, is as strong as mine.

For me the image of creativity has come to be a cupped, but open hand. Not a hand that lies extended and flat. Ideas would roll off such a surface. And certainly not a clenched fist. What could survive such a tight grasp? But a gently cradling palm, turned up to expose what it holds to the light.

When I worry, when I fret, when I try to drive a story home, my ideas seem mundane and wooden. But when I pick up an idea gently over and over again and hold it open to the air, it often learns to fly. And what flies always comes back to roost.

Tests have been devised to demonstrate creative thinking, and frankly, when I try my hand at them I rarely do well. I clench because I am too determined to prove myself *creative*. But there is one in particular, I think, that illustrates perfectly my thoughts on creativity. The assignment is as follows: Draw a triangle that touches all four sides of a square.

At first, of course, the task feels impossible, but it can be done, and the completed figure looks like this:

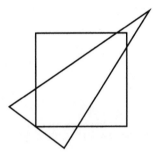

The trick, of course, is to let go of all preconceptions and allow yourself to reach outside the square.

All creativity is like that. It is a combination of persistence and openness, of returning obsessively to an idea and letting the idea go . . . all at the same time.

It's a fine balance. But then *balance*, at least in my mind, is the secret ingredient necessary for all of life.

I believe we are all born with a capacity for creativity, because we are all born wanting. The trick is to focus that wanting, to hold it lightly but persistently, until we discover the creative act that most eloquently expresses our desire.

10.

One Story's Beginnings

*T*he idea for *Face to Face* also came from a newspaper story. In fact, it came from a story even more terrible than the one about the abduction. It was the story of a fifteen-year-old boy in rural Minnesota who, one day, took up an ax and killed his mother, his father, his sister, and his brother.

Anyone who reads such a story is compelled to ask the same questions. *Why? How could such a terrible thing ever have come to happen? What was going on inside that boy? What was going on inside that family?*

Though the newspaper continued to follow this story through the boy's eventual trial (he was certified as an adult) and imprisonment, my questions were never answered. I suspect the most important questions about human beings are rarely answered in the process of seeking justice. But getting further information concerning the real circumstances of the murder was of little importance to me. I didn't need more information. What was crucial to me was the idea of a boy who was so angry and so deeply hurt that he was capable of a moment of true violence. That went onto one of my shelves.

As I lived with the idea, examined it day after day, I realized very quickly that I didn't want to write about a murder. What must have been the gore of the real situation didn't interest me at all. What interested me was the boy's pain.

The real boy who killed his family must have been deeply disturbed. Perhaps his family was abusive as well. And there was a time when mental illness or child abuse might have become the focus of my story. (*Tangled Butterfly* deals with mental illness; *Foster Child* with child abuse. Both are early books.)

The more I write, however—and perhaps the older I grow, as well—the less interested I am in such extremes of human behavior as mental illness and abuse. Rather, I find myself writing about the kinds of families most of us grow up in, the kinds most of us create when we establish our own families. I write about good, caring people who are still capable, at times, of failing one another in important ways. And so I knew almost immediately that I didn't want my main character to be either mentally ill or a victim of abuse.

The newspaper story gave me an idea, but the moment that story was on my shelf I began to make it mine. The original incident was distant from my own life and experience. It was merely a newspaper story about a boy and a family I had never met. How could I bring it closer?

The first step came when I remembered something that had happened to my own son. The morning of his last day of seventh grade, Peter said to me, "Mom, I can't go to school today."

"Why not?" I asked.

"Because," he explained, "some of the kids are going to have firecrackers, and they're going to be throwing them, and I'm scared."

It was one of those moments every parent has experienced, a moment when there seems to be no right answer. In seventh grade, Peter was small for his age, and he occasionally did get picked on. If there were going to be kids throwing firecrackers in the halls, I knew that he might indeed find himself at the wrong end of one. On the other hand, Peter had always hated school. He was very bright and very bored, and any permission to stay home simply encouraged him to find other reasons for not going. So I took a deep breath and said, "I'm sorry, Peter. You have to go."

I don't know what the rest of that day was like for Peter, but I remember very clearly what it was like for me. Filled with trepidation, I thought of him constantly. Had I made the right decision? What if there *were* firecrackers? What if he was hurt? The moment finally came that I had been waiting for. The school bus arrived, and Peter burst through the back door. I was there to greet him to see if he was all right, and I found him simply ecstatic. School was out. He had the entire summer ahead of him. Life was great!

"Did any of the kids have firecrackers?" I asked him tentatively.

"Oh, yeah," he replied with a shrug.

"Were they throwing them?" I persisted.

"Sure," he said. But none had been thrown at him, so what did it matter?

Peter is an adult now, and a parent himself, and I've never asked him if he remembers those firecrackers on the last day of seventh grade. But whether he does or not, I remember them, and the memory gave me the opening of *Face to Face*.

Let me explain. Michael, the main character in *Face to Face*, is *not* patterned after my son, Peter. I have never written a story about one of my children—or anyone else I know—and I never will.

When my daughter was eleven or so, she used to say to me, "Mom, write a story about me. You could call it *Heavens to Elisabeth*."

And I always replied, "Beth-Alison, I can't write a story about you. I don't know you well enough."

"Oh, Mom!" she would say in that tone of disgust eleven-year-olds are so good at. She was certain I was simply being stubborn, the way mothers so often are, but the truth is I didn't know her well enough to use her as a character in one of my stories.

Now, I suppose I do know Beth-Alison as well as most mothers know their daughters. She and I have always been good friends. But that's not enough to make her one of my characters, especially a main character, the one I must be able to know from inside. If I am going to write someone's story, I must look out through that person's eyes, hear with his ears, think with her thoughts, feel with his feelings. And there is only one person through whose eyes and ears and thoughts and feelings I have ever experienced the world. That person is I, myself. So Michael's story, which began with a newspaper clipping and picked up some details along the way from my son, had to take a giant step closer to me before it could ever be written.

It takes me anywhere from six months to two and a half years to write one of my novels. That doesn't mean that for six months to two and a half years I work occasionally on my novel. It means that for that length of time I sit down every day, at least five days a week, and work on that particular story until it is finally finished. If I am going to work on anything that intensively and for that long, it had better feel *important*. And the only way I know to find stories that feel truly important to me is to find ones that, for some reason, reach deeply into my own life.

How did I achieve that with *Face to Face*? Let's look at the novel more closely. Michael has two desires. One is to connect with his father, whom he hasn't seen since he was five years old. (I don't have to explain how that one is a fit for me. I've already talked about my search, through many stories, for a connection with a parent.) But Michael is also extremely angry about being picked on and convinced that he could solve all his problems if only he had a gun. How could I, a middle-aged woman who has never owned a gun, never desired to own one, and fired one very few times in her life, connect with that?

The key to Michael's story, however, isn't his longing for a gun. It is what lies beneath that longing . . . his rage, his sense of humiliation and impotence. That's the point where I needed to be able to connect. If I could feel Michael's anger, then it wouldn't be difficult to enter into the psyche of a thirteen-year-old boy and imagine a gun as his idea of a solution. It might even be relatively easy if the final moments of the story proved, as I strongly believe, that the gun wasn't the answer at all.

So again, I searched my own feelings and discovered a reservoir I had rarely touched before . . . at least not in so direct a way. That reservoir was filled with an almost forgotten impotence and humiliation and rage. It was the impotence and humiliation and rage of my own twelve- and thirteen-year-old self.

I was an outsider throughout elementary school, as I have already mentioned. I was a reasonably good student and I usually got along well with my teachers, but I had few friends among my classmates. Thus, when my mother suggested, at the end of sixth grade, that I should consider transferring to another public school for the next two years, I didn't argue.

My mother felt that the schools in the town where she taught kindergarten were better than the one in our own town. Frankly, I wasn't terribly interested in whether another school might be better, but I was interested in having a chance to start over socially with my classmates. I had, after much thought, figured out everything I had ever done to alienate myself, and this new environment, where no one knew I was supposed to be a nerd, would give me a chance to redeem myself.

So I agreed to the change, and then I spent the summer between sixth and seventh grades dreaming about how wonderful everything was going to be in my new school. I would be a cheerleader. The most popular girl in school. Everyone would love me!

A person doesn't have to know a whole lot about small towns—or for that matter about seventh-grade girls—to guess what happened. If I had been an outsider in my hometown school, that was nothing to where I found myself in the new one.

In the first place, I was now a teacher's brat, something I'd never been before. (No one in the old school knew my mother as a teacher.) In the second place, even some of the teachers looked at me with resentment and suspicion. *Why is she going to school with us when she doesn't live here?* Most important, though, *I* hadn't changed. I was still socially backward, awkwardly self-conscious, immature, a dreamer. I remember, in fact, saying to myself after I had been in the new school for a short time, *If you're the problem, moving doesn't help, because you just take yourself with you.*

Those two years were, beyond any doubt, the worst of my life. I belonged nowhere. There was an unwritten rule among the girls that no girl could go into the classroom until a group were ready to walk in together. (There might be a *boy* or, even worse, *boys* already in there!) And of course, I had no one to walk in with me. If I went into the lavatory where groups of girls chattered in front of the mirrors, all talk stopped. When I walked out again, the room erupted in laughter. Every morning and after every recess and after lunch, I stood in front of my locker, pretending to be endlessly busy sorting through papers and books. I sat by myself to eat lunch. Time on the playground was a torment.

I had one friend, the girl who had been at the bottom of the class socially before I arrived. And I remember times with her fondly, especially outside of school. But I also remember the moments in school when the more popular girls beckoned her. As hungry for acceptance as I was, she scurried to their side, even joining in their talk against me, until they grew weary of their game and dropped her again.

I used to tell myself that if the situation was reversed I would have remained loyal to our friendship. When I was being entirely honest with myself, however, I knew that I, too, would probably have gone running if the more popular girls had called. I was never tested, though, because they never summoned me.

It wasn't until those two painful years were behind me and I entered high school that the change I had been seeking finally began to come. The four-year high school I attended was large, drawing from several surrounding towns, including my own. I discovered that I could be nearly invisible there, which was infinitely preferable to being the butt of every joke. And not long after that I found a place where I truly belonged, on the yearbook staff.

I not only worked my way up to being editor by my senior year, I wrote the scripts for and directed the talent shows the yearbook staff sponsored. Those shows were among the most popular events of the school year. It was like finding a world within a world, one that was made just for me.

It is, I suppose, both ironic and unsurprising that as an adult I have become a writer who writes primarily for and about twelve- and thirteen-year-old kids. Ironic because that old pain has now become a source of creative energy. (I have heard it said that scar tissue is the toughest tissue in the body, and that must be true psychologically also.) Unsurprising because, as I've said before, the best creative energy often comes from pain, from those unresolved issues we are compelled to explore again and again.

Prior to writing *Face to Face*, however, I had never used that specific situation—the kid who was an outcast at school—in one of my books. Perhaps it was finally safe to do so precisely because Michael was so clearly not me. First, he was a boy. He lived on a dairy farm, not in a small town. (I knew a bit about dairy farms from our summer vacations at the farm, but life there was very different from growing up next to the cement mill.) He was from a divorced family. Even his love for guns helped separate him from me.

I probably would have found it difficult to write a story about a girl who was an outcast at school. That would have called up the old feelings too strongly; even now I look back with real discomfort at the awkward and unappealing person I was then. So I would have had a hard time liking any thirteen-year-old girl I drew from my own experience. And if I don't like my main character, who will?

But Michael, with his very overt anger and his longing for a gun, was different enough from me to make it safe for me to explore through him my own leftover feelings of humiliation and anger.

An author of adult fiction, Doris Betts, has said, "All one needs to write a story is one feeling and four walls." If I had to do without one or the other, I would give up the four walls. I could, conceivably, write without the comfort and security of shelter. But without a strong feeling, there would be no story at all.

And so *Face to Face* began with a newspaper story, passed through my memory of a day in my son's seventh-grade life, and ended up, finally, in the same place most of my other stories begin. Deep inside my own twelve- and thirteen-year-old self.

I have come to be grateful to that awkward, unhappy girl. She has given me so much!

11.

Beginning with the Ending

Each of my stories begins with my own understanding of—in fact, my strong empathy with—my main character's problem. In the case of *Face to Face*, that meant beginning with Michael's impotence and rage. But before I could put down a single word, I had to know exactly what kind of dramatic moment Michael's rage would lead to, and how it would be resolved.

When I decide upon the ending of my story, I am deciding upon its theme . . . what it means to me and what it will mean to my readers. And that decision is rarely difficult. It is, in fact, the resolution of the story problem and the feelings connected to that resolution that supply the energy for writing the entire novel.

I have known writers who skip around in the early stages of writing a novel, writing this scene and that from various points in the story, discovering, through this process, the shape of the whole. I always write linearly, one chapter after another, circling back constantly to make sure that the foundation I am building on is sound.

I always know my concluding scene intimately before

I begin writing—at least I know where I want my main character to be at the very end of the story—but I would never skip ahead and write the end before I reached it in the steady progression of the first draft. If I did, I might never write the story. It is the desire to experience that resolution myself, to feel that moment of release following the story's climax, that energizes the writing of the entire piece.

My decision about how to end *Face to Face* came easily. What I wanted to write about, I knew, was a boy whose sense of enraged impotence would build and build until he was *almost* capable of a moment of real violence. Because I don't believe that violence is the answer to any kind of problem, I knew that I wanted him to confront his capacity for violence and then choose to turn away.

I have heard a few writers say that they write their stories in order to discover the endings. If they knew the ending in advance, they say, they probably wouldn't bother to write the story. There is no reason to doubt that these people speak the truth of their own experience. Still, I am convinced that a writer must know the ending, subconsciously if not consciously, to begin writing at all. After all, it is the resolution that gives direction to every moment of the story from the very first line.

Because I may work more consciously, more analytically, than some writers, I know my story's ending almost before I know anything else. In *Face to Face*, I knew that Michael would turn away from the violence he was intending. I also knew that he would be reconciled with Dave, his stepfather. (Familiar stuff, of course.) What I didn't know was what his moment of near violence would entail.

Except for creating extra work for me as I stumbled my way toward a deeper understanding of my story, not knowing the details of the story's climax didn't matter. And perhaps those authors who speak of "discovering" the ending in the process of writing are speaking of the moment of climax, not of the final truth of their stories. I usually have to think I know the climax in order to begin writing, but sometimes my character discovers a better climax by the time we arrive there. Or, as was the case with Michael's story, sometimes the climax I have in mind proves not to lead effectively to the story's truth.

Through the writing of the first draft of *Face to Face*, I thought that Michael would come home in a rage and face down his family with the gun he had so longed for. Then, before he actually fired, he would choose to put the gun aside. When I wrote that long-awaited scene, however, I found myself stopped abruptly at its conclusion, unable to move on. I was incapable of writing the next chapter, in which Michael would get past that terrible moment with his family cowering before the gun to the reconciliation my story demanded. I showed what I had done to a writer friend, and she shook her head and said, "Marion, there is no place for this boy to go from here except to a mental hospital." Which, of course, wasn't what I wanted. And yet I knew that the ending I had in mind was right.

I rethought and reworked the climactic scene, moving

on this time to the end I had always intended, and then sent the story to Jim Giblin, my editor at Clarion. Now I had Michael hide out in the loft of a neighbor's barn and, secretly, hold a gun on the boy who had been his primary tormentor at school. Without ever being discovered, Michael decided to put the gun down. He turned away from the violence and, when the coast was clear, began to walk toward home. A reconciliation with and new acceptance of his stepfather was in his thoughts.

I believed this ending worked, or I wouldn't have sent it to my editor. But when Jim reported back to me, he said many of the same things my friend had said about the earlier ending. "You haven't created a character who is disturbed enough to do such a thing," he told me. "You must rethink either your character or your ending."

I could have gone back through the manuscript and built a case for Michael's being truly disturbed, not just normally miserable, but I didn't want to do that. That wasn't the boy who was in my heart. So after some further struggle, I decided, once more, to rethink the ending. What mattered, I knew, wasn't the nature of the violence Michael confronted. What mattered was the moment when he turned away from the gun as the solution to his problems.

So in the final version, Michael holds the gun on himself and then, without any intervention, chooses to put it down and turn to his stepfather. This act, Jim and I decided, fit both the story and the character I had built.

It would be possible to say that the ending of the

story changed three times. It would even be possible to say that I had to write the story in order to discover the ending. And yet the significance of the ending never wavered. Proof of this is that the revisions I did in the climactic scene required little—if any—revision of the rest of the story.

Primarily what I know, what I *must* know if I am to write any story, is what the moment of resolution will feel like. It isn't even necessary that I define the meaning of the resolution for myself. In fact, it is very likely that I won't have done so before I write. For example, when I was planning to write *Face to Face* I never said to myself that I was going to make a statement against violence, though the story does, indeed, make such a statement.

But stories are not about stating such truths, however important these truths may be. They are about living a truth through experiencing it, and it is the experience that makes the story, not the statement of its theme. The writer who starts out with an idea to express rather than a feeling to play out has the cart before the horse and will probably end up writing a sermon instead of a story. Sermons are fine in church, but masked as stories they fail every time.

I receive numerous letters from young readers, many of them clearly teacher-directed, and too often those letters reveal how my novels have been discussed in the classroom. "When I read *On My Honor*," students will say, "I learned never to go swimming in a river." Or "When I read *Rain of Fire* I learned never to tell a lie." I am often tempted to write back and say, "The heck you did!"

Because of my respect for the students who have labored over their letters and the teachers who are trying to introduce good novels into the complex demands of their days, I don't do that. But my knowledge of fiction tells me that what my readers really receive from my stories is much less easily defined. A more meaningful response came from a girl who wrote, obviously without the insistence or assistance of any teacher, to tell me that, even though she didn't usually like to read, she had cried when she had read *On My Honor*. "It's almost like it was teaching me something," she concluded, "but I don't know what."

Wonderful! I thought. *She gets it!*

ૐ

The heart of any story lies in its resolution, and the resolution will come, more directly than any other part, from my heart. Each story I write expresses what I know, what I believe, what is important to me. It will express those things whether I have thought about them consciously or not. This happens because each time I sit down to write, I am taking charge of the world, at least one small part of it. I am seeing that, this time at least, it comes out right.

So almost before I can know anything else about the story I am planning, I have to know what my character's final moments will feel like. Therein lies my story's truth.

With Michael, I wanted to face into rage—my own unacknowledged rage?—and come through to the other side. I wanted, as well, for Michael to reach out, yet again, for that parent who figures in so many of my stories, and to be accepted. Thus I knew before I wrote the first line what my ending was going to feel like, what it would mean.

We all stumble through our days, trying, however imperfectly, to meet deep and important needs. At least in fiction the destination can be sure.

12.

Finding the Middle

I have identified the sources for the ideas behind several of my novels and sorted the process for moving from idea to story. What I have not yet done is discuss the ways in which I fill in the details of plot . . . or find the middle.

Every story begins for me with knowing my main character and his or her problem. When I find that point of connection between me and my main character, I have also found the point of energy that will allow my story to build, to gather richness.

By creating a history that makes that character distinct from my own life and experience, I give myself the freedom to begin to imagine solutions to my main character's problem, solutions that will probably be quite different from anything that has ever happened in my own life. And when I know what the solution to my main character's problem is, I know what the theme of my story will be and, incidentally, why I am writing it in the first place. What remains, then, is to fill in the yawning chasm between my character's problem and its solution, the what's-going-to-happen-along-the-way of the story's development.

The development of *Face to Face* provides a good example of the way I work. From my very earliest conception of that novel, Michael lived on a farm. There were a couple of different reasons for this choice. The first, and most obvious, was that the boy in the original newspaper story had lived on a farm. So when I began to develop my story, I was already thinking about farms.

The reason I stayed with this setting, however, had to do with my own fond memories of the farm in southeastern Minnesota that my great-grandfather had homesteaded, where my mother had grown up and where I had spent summer vacations as a child. It was a dairy farm during the years I knew it best, and I can still see and smell and feel many of the details of those summer visits. As other aspects of my stories spring from a core of my own strong feelings, the setting must also come from a place that is familiar to me and important in some way as well. The idea of using a dairy farm similar to the one I had once known, set amidst the bluffs of southeastern Minnesota, answered that need.

Thus in the early stages of preparing to write *Face to Face* I set out to refresh myself about the background for my new story. I had, after all, not been on a dairy farm since I was in my teens. So I requested help from the cousin who continues to work the family farm. Since he is no longer dairying, I asked if he could arrange for me to visit some of his neighbors who were. He made the arrangements, and Ann and I set off for the southeastern part of the state.

My first discovery was that dairy farms still smelled exactly the way I remembered. The second discovery, which came almost immediately after, was that farming is a rich and complex life, a culture all its own. Despite my childhood memories, I knew that my understanding of that culture was very limited. After some thought, I decided that I could gather enough information from my cousin and his very helpful neighbors to have my main character come from a farm, but if I tried to stay there for the entire story, I would probably be in trouble. It became clear, then, that the central part of the story needed to take place away from the farm.

Michael had grown up on a farm, I decided, but his father had left when he was only five. (Remember, I was creating Michael's history with an eye toward justifying the anger that would fuel the story. Michael's being tormented by his classmates in seventh grade would not be enough. My story had to reach much deeper than that into the sources of his rage.) I decided, also, that though Michael's mother had remarried and though her husband had officially adopted Michael, Michael had continued to long for his "real" father. And that was what the center of the story would involve: Michael would go to his father and, because I already knew that my story was to be about his escalating disappointment and rage, fail to make the connection he needed there.

Next, I had to figure out where Bert, Michael's birth father, was. Not on another farm, because if I made that choice, I would immediately find myself back in a setting that I didn't really know. Not close by in Wisconsin or Iowa or another part of Minnesota, either. That would make it hard to believe that Michael wouldn't have seen his father even once in the past eight years. I had to choose a place that was distant from Minnesota, but one I already knew and could return to with relative ease. Colorado came to mind fairly quickly. I had once spent a summer in the mountains of southern Colorado working on a small dude ranch, so I had a place to begin.

At first I thought that the action between Michael and his father would center on a gun and hunting, though I knew I would have to learn about both. But as I was studying a travel brochure with an eye to returning to Colorado to refresh my memory of the state, I came across an ad for whitewater rafting. An idea hit. Wouldn't it be perfect to make Michael's father a guide on a whitewater rafting operation? That was certainly a macho enough activity to fit the needs of my story. Also, using whitewater rafting would keep me from having to rely so heavily on unfamiliar material about guns and hunting.

The problem, however, was that I knew even less about whitewater rafting than I did about guns and hunting. So I did what I always do when I need to learn about something. I paid a visit to the library and came home with an armload of material. I read and read and read until I had all kinds of technical information. What I couldn't get, however, from words on a page was the feel of the raft on the water. At least I couldn't feel it the way I needed to in order to make Michael's experience convincing.

So I returned, once more, to the ad for the Colorado company dedicated to taking tourists whitewater rafting on the Arkansas River. "It can't hurt to get some information," I said, and so I sent for a brochure and, when it came, read it with fascination . . . and rising anxiety. *What a great way to get background for my story!* I told myself. But was I brave enough to do it? I, who have always been a physical coward? Finally, I decided to call the number listed on the brochure . . . just to check.

I'm not sure whether the woman who answered the phone was incredibly convincing or if I was simply desperate to find my story's middle. Perhaps it was a bit of both. But before I had talked to her for more than ten minutes, I found myself signing up for their three-day trip, the most grueling one they offered.

"Do you want to paddle?" she asked.

"Heavens, no," I told her. "I want to be taken care of the whole way."

"You will start out your trip in Brown Canyon," she told me, which sounded fine. But then she asked, "On the third day, do you want to go through the Royal Gorge?"

Now, I had read about the Royal Gorge. The brochure had described it as "the most fierce rampaging froth in the state . . . a continuous seven-mile stretch of thunderous rapids . . . with no take-outs and very few eddies." Most of the rapids were rated four and five. (Six, in the western system of rating rapids, is considered unrunnable.)

"Uh," I stammered, my rush of determination faltering, "how bad is it?"

"Oh, by the third day you'll be ready," the woman said blithely.

Lady, I thought, *you haven't answered my question.*

But while I am not a daring person, I am also not inclined to do things by halves, so I took a deep breath and said in my bravest voice, "Sure, sign us up for the Royal Gorge." Then I went to tell Ann what it was we would be doing.

I spent the next several months thinking about my character and his problem. I also spent it thinking about *my* problem, the whitewater rafting trip that was coming up. On one occasion, I was having dinner with a group of librarians in California, and I found myself mentioning the anticipated and dreaded trip. One of the women, who seemed to be about my age and didn't look all that much braver than I felt, leaned toward me, her face glowing. "Oh, you'll love it!" she exclaimed. "I've been whitewater rafting, and it's absolutely wonderful."

I settled back into my chair, sighing with relief. So . . . everything was going to be all right.

But then she added, a bit more soberly, "Come to think of it, though, there was one man in our group who had to be tied into the raft on the second day."

I gasped, "Tied into the raft?"

She nodded. "He was so frightened after our first day out that when the second day came he refused to get back into the raft. The only way they could keep him there, once they managed to get him in, was to tie him down."

My imagination reeled. I had been playing out rafting disasters in my head for months, all of which fell considerably short of my being forced into the raft and *tied* there. What was I letting myself in for? Maybe I didn't need to write this book, after all. Surely there was some better way to make a living. As a checker at one of the local grocery stores, perhaps? Going whitewater rafting wouldn't be a requirement for that.

I returned home from California, shaken, and shortly afterward I happened to be having dinner with a writer friend who is an outdoorsman. I thought, *I'll bet Jon knows all about whitewater rafting. He'll tell me it's going to be all right.* And so I relayed the story I had just heard. Unfortunately, I didn't also explain that he was supposed to reassure me.

"Oh yes, I've heard of something like that happening," Jon said cheerfully. "This guy was so terrified after his first day of whitewater rafting that the next morning he wouldn't get into the raft again. When they tried to force him, he picked up an ax from the campsite and held everyone off with it."

"What did they do?" I asked, not sure I wanted to know.

Jon was enjoying his story more every minute. He grinned. "The only way out of where they were was by raft or helicopter. So they had to radio for a helicopter, and of course the guy had to pay for it. Do you know how expensive helicopters are?"

All my bones went soft. I didn't care, in the least, how expensive helicopters might be, though I could certainly imagine preferring one to a raft. And it was no consolation at all that, at least in my limited survey, it always seemed to be men who were struck with terror. Being a woman and socialized to conformity, I knew I would die with a cooperative smile on my lips before I would ever disrupt the trip for anyone else. But dead is still dead!

However, when I returned to Michael's story and

tried to think of some other kind of action to fill out the middle, I came up with nothing. This foolish boy *wanted* to go whitewater rafting.

Ann kept encouraging me. I would say things like, "But I can't even stand roller coasters, and nobody ever gets dumped from them." And she would reply, "But there's no reason to go on a roller coaster. There's a reason for doing this." Whereupon I would have to agree that there was, of course, a very good reason for going whitewater rafting. And so the day came when we flew to Colorado.

Carol, our guide for the first two days, was a former junior-high English teacher. (Being a junior-high English teacher struck me as perfect preparation for being a whitewater rafting guide.) And the first thing I discovered was that I *would* be doing paddle assist. I had a choice, I found, between sitting in the front and paddling, and sitting alone in the back of the raft in what could be called the ejection seat. With great trepidation, I chose to help with the paddling, which Ann was doing as well. The other woman on our trip, a nurse from Texas, gallantly took up the rear.

I could make up all kinds of fantastic adventure stories about that first day. I am a fiction writer, after all. But the truth is that it went smoothly. The sun was bright. The rushes of icy water, merely refreshing. The rapids actually fun. On the quiet stretches between the sections of whitewater, I found myself, incredibly, getting restless, actually looking forward to the next bit of action.

I started out on the second day, in front for paddle

assist again, my spirits high. No one was going to have to tie me into any raft! Around the edges, though, I was a bit worried. Was this whole experience going to be too tame to give me the kind of material that would be useful for my book?

About one hundred yards down the river from our first launching, the raft bumped against a small rock. Marcia, the nurse, was sitting alone in the back again and, in the relatively quiet water, not yet holding on. She, like me, must have been feeling on top of this whole thing. When the raft jolted, however, she made a small, inarticulate sound and tipped backward into the rushing water.

What the Arkansas River lacks in depth, it makes up for in speed. Marcia stood up to walk to shore. The force of the water knocked her down. She leaned back into her life jacket and let the current carry her, as we had been instructed to do. The river tumbled her along unceremoniously. Ann and I watched, our mouths gaping, our hands gripping our own safety line.

It took some doing to restore Marcia to the raft, but once she was back in place, scraped and shivering and rather abashed, her abrupt lesson stayed with us for the rest of the day. In fact, we reluctantly relaxed our white-knuckled grip on the safety line only when Carol commanded, "Paddle!"

"Paddle forward!" she would call as we started into the second day's heavier rapids. And we would paddle as though our very lives depended on it, because we knew by then that they did.

Even so, I didn't feel true panic until the moment in

the midst of fierce rapids when Carol cried, "Forward! Harder, harder, harder!" This was followed by a sudden lurch, a cracking sound, and then her clipped command, very calm under the circumstances, "Keep paddling. It's all yours!" Ann and I kept paddling!

It was only when we had come through to the relative calm of the other side that we understood what had happened. One of Carol's oars had gotten caught between two rocks, and when the movement of the raft finally dislodged it, the blade had been bent at a quite useless forty-five-degree angle.

After we had emerged on the other side of the rapids, Carol gave a victorious shout. I sank into the bottom of the raft, all my bones jellied. In that moment, I understood exactly how a thirteen-year-old boy, attempting to impress his rather macho father, might be humiliated in the course of a whitewater rafting trip. I also understood that on such a river, disaster is always waiting—that it is, in fact, the desire to court disaster that brings true boatmen back to the river day after day.

I understood, too, that I would never be a boatman of any stripe.

The next day we successfully navigated the Royal Gorge, including a seven-foot falls named Sunshine. (The rapids have names like The Grateful Dead and The Widowmaker, but when you go over a seven-foot falls, they call it Sunshine.) But despite the "fierce rampaging froth," which was certainly fierce and rampaging and was, unquestionably, froth, the Royal Gorge was, in some ways, anticlimactic. I had what I needed from two brief moments in the previous day . . . when I watched

Marcia go into the water and when Ann and I were left paddling on our own. I went home ready to write *Face to Face*.

I don't want to give the impression that a writer can't write about danger without first living through it. If that were the case there would be few adventure stories on the shelves. But if I am going to keep my stories fresh, I do, sometimes, need to extend my experience. And I find that I must have a base from which to begin to understand any physical experience. For instance, I didn't need to come close to drowning in order to write the scene in *On My Honor* in which Joel searches for Tony in the river and is nearly pulled under himself. But I had to have enough experience of swimming to be able to imagine how it would feel.

I am very good at asking questions, and on the white-water rafting trip, I asked questions the entire way. At one point, when we were in relatively quiet water, Carol pointed to a large boulder in the middle of the river and a swirl of water just below it. "See that eddy?" she said. "If I pulled over into it, it would take the raft and pull it down and spin it at the same time. If you were off balance, you could easily be thrown out, and then the water would take you down, hold you there for a few seconds, then pop you up again. Do you want me to show you?"

I didn't. I was perfectly willing to take her word for the entire thing. But when I wrote *Face to Face*, I used exactly that scenario. Then I sent the manuscript to her so she could check my facts.

٢

When I find my main character, his problem, his history, and the resolution to that problem which will be the story's theme, I have found the heart of my novel. The structure of the novel, chapter by chapter, comes from following my character's struggle. And sometimes that struggle also becomes mine as I try to find a means of carrying my character through from problem to resolution.

The facts that make the middle of a story possible can be as simple as a memory of setting out to run away. They can come from a combination of reading and experience, as in the birth of Nimue's pups in *Shelter from the Wind*. They can be as accidental as my discovery of a half-eaten kitten in a new litter, which provided the inspiration for *A Question of Trust*. Or they can be as carefully sought out as a whitewater rafting trip or time spent wandering among the islands in southeastern Alaska, which I have recently done in anticipation of a new novel.

The middle is often the hardest part of any piece of writing. Beginnings are technically complex, but fun. Endings are enormously satisfying. I write my stories in order to have the privilege of putting down those final words. But the middle chapters of a novel can stretch before me like a drought-stricken prairie, waiting for rain.

Over the years I have discovered, however, that by reaching a little, by opening my life to new possibilities—even scary ones—I can sometimes be my own rainmaker.

My next exploration will be a whale-watching trip off

Vancouver Island. We'll travel with a naturalist and study orcas. There is, I am certain, a killer whale out there just waiting to flesh out the middle of that story about a sibling left behind after a boy's abduction.

The whale will, I hope, be very polite when I meet him, but still just challenging enough to give me some new ideas.

13.

Back to the Beginning

"How did you get started writing?" Whether the question comes from a student or from a reporter during an interview, it always gives me pause. It's a little like being asked, "When did you first hum a tune?" or even, "How did you learn to breathe?"

I suppose what the questioner really wants to know is, "How did you first get published?" which is another topic entirely. No one "gets started writing" by getting published. I prefer to begin at the beginning.

I remember the day I discovered that I could read. My mother and I had brought a book home from the library, and I was sitting on the couch, waiting impatiently for her to come read it to me. When she continued to be busy, I finally opened the book myself—I can still remember its exact size and shape, feel its weight in my hands—and examined the print. To my great astonishment, the marks on the page separated themselves into words, words I knew.

I don't think I was especially precocious. In fact, I suspect that I was already in the first grade when my moment of discovery came. I presume I had been unlocking words in my school reader for some time. Until that moment, however, I simply hadn't made the connection between Dick and Jane and Sally, Spot and Puff and Tim—the subjects of early readers in those days—and books in general.

Learning to write, however, was a more gradual process, one in which I remember few epiphanies. There was little emphasis on "creative" writing when I was in school . . . or on writing in general, except for penmanship. (My penmanship was always poor.) But I seemed to be one of the few students in my classroom who enjoyed doing the writing that was assigned. When the teacher said, "Now, class, we're going to write," everyone groaned loudly. So of course, I groaned along with all the rest, "Do we really have to write?" After all, I didn't want to seem to be even more of a nerd than they already knew me to be. But inside I was always saying, "Great! We get to write!"

Nonetheless, the physical process of putting words on paper was and still is tedious for me. I suspect that my eye-hand coordination wasn't especially good, and even today I have little patience for any kind of activity that requires fine muscle control. I wonder sometimes if all of the keyboards were suddenly to disappear off the face of the earth and I were compelled to go back to using a pencil and paper, would my career as a writer be over?

So, even though my head was perpetually full of stories, it wasn't until I entered high school and discovered the delicious freedom of typing that I began, for the first time, to think of fiction writing as a career. Until then, when asked what I wanted to be, I always said, "A poet."

Poems, you see, are short; they don't take so much effort to write down.

In high school, I began keeping a journal (loose pages that I typed and kept in a folder), and I wrote long letters to distant friends and relatives as well. I even made carbon copies of my typewritten letters, unwilling to see my words vanish into the mail. But I still wasn't writing the stories I loved.

Part of the reason was that the stories I constantly spun in my head were so complex that I didn't know how to begin to put them down on paper. In fact, I wrote only one short story during all of high school. It was a rather melodramatic piece about a young ballerina (I studied dance throughout my girlhood) who was revealed, at the last moment of the story, to be blind. I submitted it for a contest in a teen magazine but it didn't win, though I was convinced it should have. (I can still remember the one that did with great clarity. The story of a girl coming upon an automobile accident that involved her own parents, it may have been as melodramatic as mine, but was written, as I recall, with some real sophistication.)

Throughout school, teachers encouraged me to write. My parents, however, took little interest in what I was putting on paper, beyond being satisfied that I was performing as expected in school. The idea that I might become a writer must have seemed as remote to them as if I had talked of being a rock star one day. But I had an aunt, my mother's oldest sister, who was a poet and the editor of a poetry column for her community newspaper in Ohio, and she showed real interest in my work.

Perhaps even more important to me than her encouragement, though, was the example she set. Aunt Dyllone took her own writing seriously. She took it so seriously that, though she was the mother of four sons and from a generation in which being mother and wife was supposed to be sufficient career for any woman, she rented a room in town and escaped there regularly to work on her poems and her column. Virginia Woolf, a famous writer born only a few years before my aunt, wrote of a woman's need to have "a room of one's own." Few women of their generation ever had one, though, and I was struck with something close to awe when I heard of my aunt's hideaway. There was no telephone in it, I was told, and no one was allowed to interrupt her when she was there. When I considered my aunt, there could be no question. Writing was *important*!

I married young, before I had even finished college, but went on to complete my degree while my husband completed his. I never quit writing, but for many years my time at the typewriter was forced into whatever cracks were left after all the "important" things were done. I became a graduate assistant, teaching freshman composition at the University of Oklahoma, and then went on to teach in a Wisconsin high school while my husband, Ron, studied at an Episcopal seminary nearby.

From those years I remember most the piles of compositions and my hunger to be writing instead of grading them. On Saturday mornings, when the other seminarians' wives who had Monday through Friday jobs were busy cleaning their tiny apartments, I always sat down to add another page or two to my journal. I remember showing up at a friend's door about noon every Saturday with my latest words in hand. Her apartment would be spotless, but I had been *writing*!

Peter was born before we left seminary, Beth-Alison two years later in a small town in the Oklahoma panhandle. I settled into being mother and clergy wife and, as we moved from state to state, became involved in the communities in which we lived. I didn't stop writing, but it definitely took a back seat to all the other choices I had made. And I was still writing very little fiction. Mostly I continued to keep my writing muscles—those in the brain—limber with my journal and with letters.

The day came when two significant moments collided. My youngest child started first grade, and Ron came to me and said, "You know, it would be awfully nice if you'd go back to work and earn some money."

I suddenly had a vision of myself as a very old woman lying on my deathbed complaining, "But wait a minute, I want to write. Nobody ever gave me time to write." And that was when I realized that no one ever would *give* me time to write . . . except me.

"I want to take five years," I said to him, "to work seriously and full time at my writing, as though it were a job someone is paying me to do." I promised that if I hadn't achieved something he and I could agree was success by the end of that time, I would go back to teaching, which I knew would gobble up most of my creative energy and probably end, or at least limit, my dream of ever becoming a professional writer.

We both knew that no one out there was offering to pay me two cents for anything I wrote, but still, he agreed. And so I found myself sitting in the corner of our bedroom in front of the manual Smith-Corona portable typewriter that had been my high-school graduation gift from my parents in 1956, facing the blankest sheet of paper anyone has ever looked at. I was thirty-three years old. Old enough to know that five years can fly by very swiftly. And I didn't even know what I wanted to write about, only that I was certain writing was what I wanted to do.

I began with picture-book texts. My children were young, and I had been reading picture books for years. And I thought, I'm rather embarrassed to admit now, "Anybody can do better than that!" The first thing I discovered was how very difficult "better than that" could be.

I was living in Hannibal, Missouri, at the time—Mark Twain's boyhood home—though I found little support there for writers. There was a Mark Twain Roofing Company and Mark Twain Fried Chicken, but if there were any prospective Mark Twains who were struggling to put words on a page, I never met them. There was a library, however, and I haunted it, coming home with armloads of picture books every time.

Gradually, I grew bored with picture books—which should have told me something important—and I moved up the stacks and began to choose, quite randomly, a few books for older kids. After I had read those, I wandered farther and encountered a separate shelf of Newbery Medal books. The Newbery Medal had been around for a long time, but I had never heard of it. The grade school I had attended didn't have a library, and there was certainly little emphasis in the classroom on books that weren't textbooks. But I knew by the gold medal on the jackets of these books that someone had decided they were good, so I took an armload home and began to read . . . and to fall in love.

This . . . *this* was what I wanted to write! It wasn't that I was anticipating getting the Newbery. I never dreamed of such a thing. Rather, those books challenged me, excited me, sent me back to my own writing filled with fire. I discovered, for nearly the first time, books for young people that covered a wide range of topics with honesty, integrity, and real literary skill.

The two novels that moved me most deeply on that first spate of reading were William Armstrong's *Sounder* and Paula Fox's *The Slave Dancer*. (It is ironic that both of these books are sometimes criticized today for not being politically correct. I still love them and think that some of today's demands for "correctness" are quite foolish.) Reading those novels and others like them convinced me that if a story idea felt important to me and if it could touch a child's life, I could write it without apology or excuse or pretense.

I had an eleven-year-old foster son at the time, a boy who had lived with his great-grandmother until he was placed in foster care. Mike was one of several foster children who had been part of our family at one time or another, and I had come to have strong feelings about the powerlessness of children in the foster-care system. Even more important, I had strong feelings about my own remembered powerlessness as a child, the experience of not being in charge of one's own life that every child endures. And then there was the issue that under-lies all of my stories, my own lifelong search for an understanding parent, which probably created my empa-thy with foster children to begin with. Without even knowing where it was coming from, I could tap into the energy of that old longing. And the combination of all that launched me into my first novel.

When I began to write, I stayed very close to Mike's real situation, too close. I discovered within a few pages that I needed more distance. I needed to become my main character in a way I couldn't when I was pattern-ing that character on someone I knew. And so I backed up and started again, this time making the main charac-ter a girl, creating her out of bits and pieces of Mike's situation and, more important, out of bits and pieces of myself.

Once I began to treat my writing as my work instead of as a guilty hobby, something to be squeezed in when there weren't more important needs to be met, I began to gather power. Not that I was confident what I was writing would be published. That still seemed a distant dream. But I gained respect for what I was doing simply by calling it *work*. However we may feel about the arts in this society, anything called work is considered *important*.

I found myself, for a time, thinking about going back to college to "learn how to write." I investigated the Master of Fine Arts degree in creative writing at the University of Iowa, an old and prestigious program. (When my husband had gone from the University of Oklahoma to seminary, I had abandoned a nearly completed Master's Degree in Literature.) But while I was trying to work out the logistics of traveling so far with young children at home, a thought suddenly occurred to me. If I spent the time writing that I was considering using to drive back and forth between Hannibal and Iowa City, I might actually accomplish something.

A position teaching English became available at a local college, and I found myself applying for it. But when I returned home after the interview and looked at my waiting typewriter, I called and withdrew my application.

Quite unexpectedly, I was offered a job as a child welfare worker. I had no training for such a position, but the lure of the work was strong . . . not to mention the enticement of a salary. Then I asked myself, *If you could buy anything you wanted with that money, what would it be?* And the answer came back strong and clear, *Time to do my own writing and my own reading.* Which, of course, was precisely what I would be giving up by taking any position at all.

I kept on with my writing.

We moved to Minnesota and a new parish for my husband. I quit playing Super Clergy-Wife. I had headed up the church school in our previous parish; I didn't even check the new one out. Nor did I set up an emergency call-in service for the community. Or take in foster children. Or work with youngsters in trouble with the law. In fact, in all the years I was in that parish, the people in the congregation never even discovered that I could cook. I happen to be a very good cook, but when they were looking for someone to help with church dinners, they never approached me. And I never offered. Instead, I stayed home and wrote. It was my work, after all, and I was on a deadline.

I worked as if I hadn't the slightest doubt about where I was going or whether I would get there, though I had every doubt in the world. It is difficult even to describe those doubts. I would walk into a library or a bookstore, take one look at the full shelves, and find myself flushing with embarrassment. Who did I think I was, trying to add to that store? Who would consider buying a book by a nobody named Marion Dane Bauer, anyway? Did I really think I had something to say?

I remember the first time I filled out a questionnaire—it was at a doctor's office—and put the word *writer* in the blank that asked for occupation. I found myself looking over my shoulder, waiting for someone to leap out of the shadows and accuse me of lying. I was still essentially unpublished. A couple of poems in literary magazines, a column in my hometown newspaper when I was in college, and, later, one in a church magazine hardly counted. How dare I? And yet I continued to consider my writing my work.

"Sorry. I'd *love* to bake cookies for the cub scouts, but I have to work."

"The ladies at the church are having a luncheon? That sounds nice, but I'm afraid I'll be working that day."

"Thanks for calling, but I must get back to work."

A couple of months after we moved to a suburb of Minneapolis, I saw a notice of a writers' conference to be held in St. Paul. I had just finished the first draft of

Foster Child, and I hadn't any idea where to go from there. Here was my answer.

When I arrived at the conference, I discovered that we would be allowed an unprecedented privilege—to turn in full-length manuscripts, even novels, to be read by the presenters.

Maia Wojciechowska, the Newbery-Medal-winning author of *Shadow of a Bull*, was one of the presenters. Trembling with eagerness and fear, I gave the manuscript of *Foster Child* to her. Then I waited. Maia, I knew, would be nothing if not candid: During the first couple of days of the week-long conference, I had seen her return a manuscript to another participant. "This is all a pile of s——!" she'd announced as she thrust the pages at the embarrassed writer. And everyone in the vicinity quaked.

Nevertheless, as I drove to the conference each day, a fantasy danced in my head. I couldn't stop it. When I walked into the hotel where the conference was being held, people were going to be lined up at the door, whispering to one another. "There she is!" they would say. "There's that wonderful writer Maia told us about!" My fantasy also had a flip side, which was Maia, herself, announcing what my story was a pile of. Either scenario seemed possible, because I was at that uncertain stage every developing writer goes through. I hadn't the slightest idea what value, if any, my writing had.

The last day of the conference came, and I walked into the hotel. No one was lined up. No one was whispering. I shrugged. What had I expected, after all? I didn't really believe that silly dream. Besides, deep in my heart I knew what my story was a pile of, and I'd just have to take my medicine when it was handed out. So I went into the first session, a panel discussion involving all of the presenters. I was wreathed in gloom and only half-listening to what was being said until the end of the session, when Maia stood up and walked to the microphone.

"Uh, Maia," the moderator said, "I'm afraid we're out of time."

"I can't help it," she replied. And she leaned across the podium to get closer to the mike. "I'm so excited," she told us. "I was kept awake last night." And then the most unlikely fantasy I have ever had came true. "Marion Dane Bauer," she announced, "has written a book called *Foster Child*, and it's good . . . it's going to be published!"

The rest of that day is mostly a blur in my memory, except that, very quickly, I came to understand several important truths. I knew that Maia was not easily impressed and that I could trust her judgment about my writing. At the same time, I realized that I had written on a subject very dear to her heart and that it might not be equally dear to the hearts of publishers. But for the first time I also knew—and this is what mattered—that whether or not that particular story was ever published, I would, someday, write something a publisher would want.

I barely needed to drive home that night. I could almost have lifted my arms and flown. When I arrived, I said to my family, "There will never be another moment to compare with this one." And there never has been.

There have been awards, and those have been lovely. There has been deep satisfaction, even unanticipated delight. But no moment has come close to Maia's pronouncement, because that was the first time I knew— with real certainty—that I was a writer.

And everything else follows from that.

14.

For Children . . .
For Me

I have been teaching fiction writing to adults for a couple of decades, and many of my former students are now published writers themselves. That fact is a source of great satisfaction to me. But because most of my students are writing for children, work ranging from picture books to young-adult novels, I have seen one phenomenon occur again and again. First-time children's authors are, of course, always thrilled to be published. Then very soon afterward, they are disappointed . . . and angry . . . and hurt. "Doesn't anybody value my work?" they ask me. "Isn't there anyone out there who thinks children's books matter?"

"Well, yes," I tell them. "There are teachers and children's librarians and, of course, the kids themselves. But if you are looking for prestige, if you are looking for money, even if you are only looking for respect from the world out there, you are probably in the wrong field." And that is, unfortunately, true. In our culture, work done for kids, whatever it might be, is always considered to be of less value than the same work done for adults.

When I go into schools, even students will ask me,

"But why do you write for kids?" And I know from the tone of the question that they consider it an odd thing to do. I am tempted sometimes to reply, facetiously, "Because I'm not smart enough to write for real people," which I suspect is the assumption behind the question.

But the true answer is a complex one, and I suspect it takes a slightly different form for each children's writer. I once heard a well-known writer for children say, "No one ever starts out intending to write for children. They just discover, along the way, that that's where their writing fits." If what he said is true, then I must be the exception, because I did start out with a young audience in mind. And although I have taken some side trips along the way—including writing an adult play, a chancel drama called *God's Tears: a Woman's Journey*—children have always been the primary audience I have sought.

Why? I suppose it has something to do with liking kids. In fact, I find that I like most kids better than I like most adults. I like talking with them and being with them. (One of the nicest compliments I ever received was from a young friend who once told me that I wasn't "like a regular adult.") But my call to write for young people goes well beyond that. For whatever reasons—and I know the reasons only imperfectly—thinking about childhood gives me energy.

Events in children's lives feel important to me in a way that those in adults' lives do not. When I go to the video store, for instance, I inevitably come home with a film that has a child at its center. (Some of the worst films ever made have a children at their centers, but I am still compelled to bring them home, again and again.)

When I turn to adult material, I find that as a woman in my fifties I have little interest in the struggles that occurred in my twenties or even my forties. They no longer seem either important or interesting. And if I consider the circumstances of my present life, I find that I haven't yet developed the perspective needed to turn them into a story. If I do try to write about my own current life issues, I find myself writing too close to the bone.

But when I return to childhood, especially those twelve- and thirteen-year-old years, I am wholly there. I can feel what each moment is like, and each moment matters. It isn't that I haven't grown beyond my twelve- and thirteen-year-old self, because, gratefully, I have. I am much more self-confident now, infinitely happier, and thus much less self-involved. For better and for worse, though, that twelve- and thirteen-year-old remains as part of the core of my personality. I cannot cast her off, and as difficult as it was to *be* her, I carry her with me still.

And yet, when I sit down to write, my adult self stays in charge, choosing the words, directing the action, so that I may speak the truths the adult has come to know. I write out of the energy of the girl's longing, but it is the woman's understanding that brings my stories to the page.

I was a "different" child, even an odd one. I am not exactly a typical adult, either, but differentness is usually dealt with somewhat more gently among adults than among schoolmates. In one of my short stories, I used an event from my early childhood that exemplifies my differentness. "Dancing Backwards," which is included in an anthology I edited called *Am I Blue? Coming Out from the Silence*, begins with the narrator's remembering a dance recital when she was four and supposed to be a sunbeam. Unable to recall where the audience would be when she sashayed in from an adjoining room, the narrator made the wrong choice and performed her entire dance with her back to the audience.

I was that four-year-old sunbeam, dancing backward before our local women's club. And it was only recently that, remembering the event, it occurred to me to wonder why I hadn't simply looked at the other little girls in the line and faced the same way they were facing. It says something important about me—then and now—that I never thought of doing such a thing.

In the adult world, that inclination to stand apart, to make my own choices, even to be different, works very well for me most of the time. Occasionally I find myself at a cocktail party or some other adult event where noisy conformity is expected, and frankly, I'm pretty miserable for the brief time I'm there. But then I escape back into my life. I sit down at my computer. I take a deep breath. And I submerge myself in the story that is waiting for me.

So, if the world isn't too impressed with children's writers, that suits me just fine. It gives me the deep privacy I need to peer into that child hole and come up with more riches.

Twenty years ago, Maia Wojciechowska praised my

work. About the same time, I began a correspondence with Madeleine L'Engle, who was generous with her support and encouragement. I found a fine editor in James Cross Giblin at Clarion Books. We have worked together so closely for so long that I don't believe either of us could sort out, any longer, what it is that he has taught me and what I have taught him. I know that though I have moved on to work with several other editors, too, the books I do with him continue to grow under his thoughtful guidance.

After twenty-eight years in a commitment that had always been a painful fit for me, I left my marriage. I continue, though, to be grateful to my former husband, not just for the five years of "the test," but for the ten which followed that. In all that time, I never came close to the teacher's salary I could have earned if I had gone "back to work," and he didn't complain. My children put up with my absorption in other worlds pretty much without complaint, too, though Beth-Alison could never understand why I wasn't willing "just to write one bestseller and get us some money."

My house is quiet now, much quieter than it was during the years when my kids and their friends were constantly tromping through. A cardinal whistles from the trees outside my study window. Sometimes Mr. Spriggan, my sheltie, barks. One of the cats climbs onto my lap, arches her back, blocking the computer screen, and purrs. (Before she will leave, Popcorn usually presses her mouth against mine in a prolonged and intense kiss. Muddle, the Devon rex, exits across the keyboard in a huff, accomplishing wondrous changes to my work-in-progress. And our Siamese, Taku-Taku, always has several comments about the state of world affairs to make before she will allow me to put her back on the floor.) I hear the garage door go up and know that Ann, my life partner, is home, and I am glad. And in that near silence, the stories only come faster.

Why do I write for children? Well, the truth is that I don't, really. If the stories I write appeal to children, that is both bonus and blessing. But I write them, actually, for a child who hasn't been seen around here for a long time. The one I write my stories for had a miserable time in seventh and eighth grades. She was the one who used to do a lot of dreaming, making story figures out of marbles and flowers and thin air. She danced backward when she was four years old, as well, and has never quite found an officially approved place since . . . except when she steps out of the line and sits down to write.

But there is no question . . . the writing is its own reward. It is the simple process of putting words down, one after another, of seeing ideas emerge, of sharing my characters' struggles, that gives my days focus and meaning. And there is no award, no fantasy of public accolade fulfilled, that can compete with the day-after-day satisfaction of work that is done with love.

I am a writer. My books sometimes touch children. My life is good.

Index of Stories and Novels Discussed

Unless otherwise identified, all are by the author.